About the Author

Brian has been a bird lover for almost his whole life. It first started with feeding the ducks in his local park in Birmingham and has since taken him to many parts of Europe and North Africa in his quest to study birds. Eighty years of experience lies behind him. Brian has taught bird study to students at both the University of Birmingham and Keele University and taken parties of bird watchers on many bird study tours in both the UK and Europe. As well as looking at birds, learn where you may see the birds…

A Young Person's Guide to Bird Watching

Brian C. George

**Cover Illustration of Mute Swan, cygnets, by Sarah
D George**

A Young Person's Guide to Bird Watching

Olympia Publishers
London

www.olympiapublishers.com
OLYMPIA PAPERBACK EDITION

A CIP catalogue record for this title is
available from the British Library.

ISBN: 978-1-80074-699-2

First Published in 2023

Olympia Publishers
Tallis House
2 Tallis Street
London
EC4Y 0AB

Printed in Great Britain

Dedication

I dedicate this book to the memory of my daughter, Sarah D George, with whom many happy hours of bird study were enjoyed.

INTRODUCTION

For a young person becoming interested in birds, life can be very confusing.

Most field guides show illustrations of large numbers of British birds, the majority of which the beginner is unlikely to see, and make an interesting hobby look very difficult. The thoughts behind this publication are to simplify things and introduce the reader to the pleasure of bird watching; the identification of rare and unusual species can come as the watcher develops.

We have decided not to illustrate this work as most readers will have computers or mobile phones and they can 'Google' all the illustrations they require and listen to the related bird calls. Knowledge of bird calls helps considerably as they are often the first sign of a bird's appearance, but calls and song are not quickly learned, so just concentrate on learning the ones you are most likely see. Learn what the blackbird sounds like, do not worry about some rarity.

As we intend this guide to be a book for the pocket, we have only written principally about the birds you are most likely to see, in your own garden, local park or woodland and on your seaside holiday, plus the few more unusual species you may come across. Once you have mastered these, you can move onto the remainder of the birds found in the British Isles, and then one of the many field guides available will become a necessity.

Most field guides list the birds in their scientific sequence and for the beginner this can be very confusing. They will not know what bird is in what family: to find a jay you have to look at the crow family; a puffin is an auk; a blackbird is a thrush; and so you could go on. We will deal with birds in strict alphabetical sequence and obviously providing the information of where and when they may be seen.

By reading this book you are starting off on a rewarding hobby that will remain with you all your life. Birds are one of the few wild creatures which can be seen all year long and seen everywhere, be it town, country or on the sea, so you are never far from a bird. You can start by feeding the birds in your own garden or park; this brings the birds in close to you and also helps the birds to survive by providing them with food, you are also doing your bit for conservation.

The only equipment needed, apart from this book is a pair of binoculars, and these need not be expensive; a pair of 8x magnification is a good start, and these can frequently be purchased second hand, a notebook and pen. I suggest that from day one you keep a record of what you see and where. You never know when this information may become important in this changing world of ours. My own records have shown how bird populations have declined or increased as the case may be and my occasional record has been of national importance.

So let us get started, and I hope you enjoy the journey as much as I have and still do. You not only meet beautiful birds on your travels, you also meet many like-minded people, who too love birds.

Before we start, here are the birds we will look at, and whilst doing so you may wish to 'Google' a few:-

Arctic Tern	Avocet
Barn Owl	Blackbird
Blackcap	Black-headed Gull
Blue Tit	Brambling
Bullfinch	Buzzard
Canada Goose	Carrion Crow
Chaffinch	Chiffchaff
Coal Tit	Collared Dove
Common Tern	Coot
Cormorant	Cuckoo
Curlew	Dunlin
Dunnock	Egyptian Goose
Fieldfare	Gannet
Goldcrest	Goldfinch
Great, Black-backed Gull	Great Crested Grebe
Great Spotted Woodpecker	Great Tit
Greenfinch	Grey Heron
Greylag Goose	Grey Wagtail
Guillemot	Herring Gull
House Martin	House Sparrow
Jackdaw	Jay

Kestrel

Kittiwake

Lapwing

Linnet

Little Grebe

Long-tailed Tit

Mallard

Marsh Tit

Moorhen

Nuthatch

Oystercatcher

Pied Wagtail

Raven

Red-legged Partridge

Redwing

Reed Warbler

Rook

Sand Martin

Shelduck

Siskin

Snipe

Sparrowhawk

Stock Dove

Swift

Treecreeper

Tree Sparrow

Waxwing

Willow Tit

Wren

Yellowhammer

Kingfisher

Knot

Lesser Black-backed Gull

Little Egret

Little Owl

Magpie

Meadow Pipit

Mistle Thrush

Mute Swan

Osprey

Pheasant

Puffin

Razorbill

Redshank

Reed Bunting

Robin

Sanderling

Sedge Warbler

Shoveler

Skylark

Song Thrush

Starling

Swallow

Tawny Owl

Tree Pipit

Tufted Duck

Willow Warbler

Woodpigeon

Yellow Wagtail.

I have also included a few of the more frequently seen escapees from collections, some of which are not included in the British List.

For size details, L is length, WS is wingspan, used as appropriate. Length: - the distance from tip of bill to tail. Wingspan: - the distance from the tip of one wing to the tip of the other wing. For the smaller birds, known as passerines, wing size is rarely stated.

CHAPTER I

THE BIRDS

ARCTIC TERN. L 33 – 35cm. WS 80 – 95 cm.
Undertakes the longest migration of all bird species. It spends the winter in the Antarctic before returning to breed, and as can be told by its name, it breeds in the far north, well into the Arctic Circle. Some do breed in the UK, in northern England and Scotland, but we, in the remainder of the UK, see it mainly as a bird of passage in spring and autumn. It is seen more often near to the coast although some do migrate well inland, calling in at our larger lakes and reservoirs where they feed on fish and other water creatures.

They are graceful birds with slender wings and forked tails, and were frequently referred to as sea swallows. This bird can be confused with the common tern, which we will deal with later, but has a smaller and darker red bill, a steeper forehead, grey underparts, rather short legs which are very noticeable when standing and longer tail streamers, which protrude beyond the wing tips.

The bird arrives April – May, and migrates July – October, the earlier birds are probably unsuccessful breeding birds.

AVOCET. L 42 – 46 cm. WS 77 – 80 mm
I have included the avocet in my list as it is a special bird which is slowly recolonising England particularly. The bird was lost as a British breeding species many years ago, but over recent years has slowly returned and now breeds in many parts of the country. For many years now, new areas of wetland have been created and the bird has moved into these and breeds as far inland as central England itself. They have now, for instance, started to breed in Birmingham.

Although they may not have been seen by large numbers of people, they are well known to many as they are the emblem of the RSPB (The Royal Society for the Protection of Birds).

They are a very elegant bird and with their black and white plumage and upcurved bill they are like no other wader. (Waders are birds commonly found along shorelines and mudflats that wade in order to find food such as insects and invertebrates.) They are very long legged and these are a bright grey in colour. They are noisy birds and their 'pleet, pleet' notes constantly ring out so, if not seen they are certainly heard. They have a distinctive feeding manner, swinging their head from side to side with the upcurved bill skimming off surface -water invertebrates. They can also swim well, having webbed toes.

Most of the birds we see are summer migrants from the Iberian peninsula and West Africa; although several over-winter on our south coast; they return to their breeding grounds March – April, leaving September – October. A most noble bird.

They are found on wetland habitats where the water is about 10 cm deep, and this can be saline or fresh water. The east coast of England is probably their favoured territory at present, although as mentioned earlier, they have moved well inland.

The avocet is one of our success stories, unlike the situation with some of our native birds.

BARN OWL. L 33 – 39 cm, WS 85 – 93 cm.
Our most well known and unmistakable owl, to many known as the 'screech owl' due to its call. A very pale looking bird with a distinctive heart shaped face and bold black eyes which stare directly ahead, but this is compensated by their head movements. They are white to yellowish-white beneath which gives them an almost ghostly appearance. In flight the wings are beaten jerkily and stiffly which provides them with a distinctive flight pattern.

They nest in lofts, hollow spaces in barns, hence their name, outhouses and hollow trees. They are a bird of open country with fields, ditches, scrub and newly planted plantations, and for many townsfolk, they have a definite association with church grounds. Barn owls hunt mainly at dawn and dusk although their calls can be heard throughout the night. They are chiefly residential, and stay in their territory for most of their life although their young do wander once they leave the nest to find territories of their own.

Our most distinctive and easily recognised owl.

BLACKBIRD. L 24 – 25 cm.

If it was not for its bright yellow bill and eye-ring, the male blackbird would be one of our few completely black birds, the female being dark brown with a slightly paler brown throat and breast. Very much a ground feeding bird and spends most of its time running around on the ground, frequently rushing under a bush for cover, usually protesting with a number of 'chak, chak' calls. Song is heard from the resident males as early as January and continues through to July. Song is best described as yodelling flute-like notes followed by a more chuckling section.

Breeds widespread over the UK, frequently in woodland, with thick undergrowth, parks, gardens and open scrub. A regular garden bird and feeds on worms, snails, insects, berries and fruits, plus food provided by people.

Although a common British bird we have many here as winter visitors from the continent, and these can sometimes be clearly identified as the males usually have a darker bill. We also have passage birds from northern Europe, which are moving southwards. Passage birds and winter visitors are usually seen late September to March.

BLACKCAP. L 14 cm.

Blackcaps are a member of the group of birds we know as warblers, many of which are among our most pleasant song birds, and the blackcap is no exception.

They are principally a summer migrant, although recently they have been seen throughout the year. This raises the question are some birds now over-wintering and becoming a resident or are these birds winter visitors from further north? During the winter period they are frequently seen in gardens on bird feeders and I have found they also love grated cheese.

Blackcaps are a large looking warbler, the male being uniformly grey looking, with a distinctive jet-black cap, hence its name, the female being more grey-brown with a dark reddish cap. They are very much a bird of the leaf canopy and not regularly seen, but well heard. Their song is a rippling melody which erupts into a loud fluting display of clear notes. Once learned it is quickly picked up. A key member of any woodland dawn chorus.

They are a woodland species, deciduous woodland with plenty of cover, although in recent years they have also come into town parks and large gardens with ground cover.

Blackcaps are early migrants from the Western Mediterranean returning late- March and leaving us August –September.

BLACK-HEADED GULL. L 38 – 44 cm, WS 94 – 105 cm.
Our commonest gull, widespread and a resident species, with passage and winter visitors. Frequents fresh waters, seashores and cultivated land. Regularly seen following the plough. People frequently refer to gulls as sea gulls, many black headed have never seen the sea and have no need to, all the food they require and nesting sites are available inland.

In full adult plumage they are a tidy looking gull with a dark brown head, red bill, red legs, a pale grey back, black primaries (wing tips), and clean white underparts. They are not so neat when in moult as they lose their brown heads which become white with dark markings round the eye and on the head.

I will not attempt to describe the call, apart from to say it is screaming and obtrusive and very grating. You would not want a colony in your own garden that is for sure.

BLUE TIT. L 11.5 cm.
If you feed the birds it is one of the most frequent birds to be seen in your garden. When I first became interested in birds, to see a blue tit meant you had to visit a piece of woodland. As we have now become a nation of bird feeders, they are a regular garden visitor.

Their blue crown, black and white face markings combined with blue on the wings and yellow underparts, makes them a colourful small bird. They are very active and vocal, their song is best described as a delightful ringing 'pseet-see-sirrrrrrrr', plus various other calls such as 'chee-dee-dee-dee',and a prolonged 'ptsee-tsee-dee-dee-dee'.

The breeding habitat is varied. Deciduous woodlands, parkland trees, and gardens, here it readily takes to nest boxes. Food is mainly insects and their larvae but in gardens it feeds readily on seed, peanuts and, in my own garden, especially on sunflower hearts. They will lay eight eggs or more, although they rarely raise that many.

They are a resident bird in the UK, but during the winter months they frequently flock up with other titmice and move out of their breeding ranges.

BRAMBLING. L 15.5 cm.

In many respects similar to our chaffinch, especially the female. In its summer plumage the male is unmistakable with the black head, orange shoulders, breast and wing bar, and in flight the white rump is distinctive on both sexes. The chaffinch has a grey or greenish rump.

They are a winter visitor to the UK, arriving September/October and have returned home to breed by May. Brambling are a northern European breeding bird, Scandinavia and eastwards, although they have occasionally bred in Scotland, but rarely.

Regular visitors to garden feeders where they are partial to peanuts, but more frequently seen in wooded areas, beech trees and hornbeams being particular favourites, feeding on the fallen seeds. They can also be seen on farm fields where they will associate with other birds. They usually form up into flocks, especially with chaffinches.

In some years we receive them in large numbers depending upon the conditions back home in their breeding territories. A bird to really look out for during the winter months.

BULLFINCH. L 16 cm.

A large and bulky looking bird, distinctive and easily identified. The male has a black cap and black bill, grey shoulders, red breast and underparts, white under tail, wings black with a white wing bar. Only four colours but put together well. The female is a paler version of the male, but still very colourful. The song is a very soft warble but when in flocks the regular call is 'chet, chet, chet', and this is quite loud.

A fairly common bird of forest edges, scrub, plantations, gardens and orchards, and in winter it often visits gardens and orchards where it consumes buds.

Because of this it can cause damage to orchards where it eats the flower buds, creating damage to commercial fruit crops, so the bird is not loved by all. In my own garden they have a preference for honeysuckle buds, but as the plant is only there for the birds, I do not mind. They encourage a most beautiful bird into my garden where they brighten up many a drab winter day.

They are a resident bird but we do get a few over- wintering birds each year from Scandinavia, and their race is slightly larger than ours and a little more bright in colour.

BUZZARD. L 51 – 57 cm. WS 112 – 128 cm.

Now probably the commonest bird of prey we see today, although that was not always the case. Several years ago their number declined dramatically due to the introduction of myxomatosis to the rabbit population. which not only killed the rabbit but also destroyed whatever ate the rabbit. Buzzards being big rabbit eaters suffered the most and were almost driven to extinction. Fortunately this was made illegal and stopped, just in time to not only save the rabbit, but also the many creatures which feed on them. Since then the buzzard has made a remarkable recovery and as mentioned earlier, is now probably our commonest bird of prey. I live in the Midlands, in Staffordshire, and if I saw two or three buzzards a year locally, that was about it, now if I do not see that many a week, something has gone wrong.

When seen closely many people believe they have seen an eagle, but it has got quite a way to go before rivalling the eagle in size, although it is certainly the largest of the common birds of prey.

They are a medium sized, predominantly dark brown bird, although some are quite pale looking. In flight they have broad rounded wings with distinctive white patches at primary bases. It soars with wings raised in a shallow 'V' and glides on flat or slightly arched wings, a most leisurely way of flying I always feel, buzzards rarely do anything in a rush. Its call is a type of mewing whistle 'peee-ay', not at all the call you would expect a bird of prey to make, but at least easily recognised, and travels some distance.

It is very widespread, common in cultivated country with groups of mature trees, bordering pasture and arable land, bogs, clearings and open terrain where it can hunt. Frequently seen on telegraph poles and bare trees from where it can survey the ground for food, which can be rodents, young birds, snakes, frogs, worms, large insects and of course rabbits. Will also feed on carrion. Unlike hawks and falcons, rarely takes birds in the air, being a ground hunter.

They are a resident bird although we do have a few summer migrants from further south, and birds from Scandinavia will either pass though the UK or over winter here, usually arriving September – November and departing north again March – April.

CANADA GOOSE. L 53 – 56 cm. WS 150 – 160 CM.

Our largest goose and probably our commonest goose. A native to North America, hence the name. There it is a migratory bird moving down from Canada to the southern states of the U.S.A. Here it has become a more sedentary bird rarely moving more than 50 km from where it was raised. Birds from across the Atlantic rarely migrate to the UK, our population is solely due to their introduction many years ago and they have found conditions ideal for breeding, and have done so very successfully.

With their big brown body and long black neck, with distinctive white cheeks, they are unlikely to be confused with any other goose. They are a common bird of city ponds where they readily come for food, and in the wild they are to be found on lakes, marshes, and in sheltered coastal bays. Frequently seen on farmland and fields where they graze. In flight are readily identified by their trumpeting 'ah-honk', very loud and carries a long distance.

Unlike grey geese which regularly fly in skeins of either a 'V' formation or long lines of geese, Canada geese are usually seen in loose but noisy flocks.

When seen in flight their long neck is a rather striking feature and if seen in silhouette helps in identification.

CARRION CROW. L 47 cm.

One of our only two completely black birds, legs, bill, eyes and plumage all black. In Scotland we have a species of our carrion crow, the hooded crow, which is a combination in colour of grey and black. They do interbreed in the areas where both can be seen.

Frequently confused with rooks, but the rook has a white bill against the black bill of the carrion crow. Confusion can occur however with juvenile birds when the young rook has a black bill. In flight look for the more squared off tail, a rook's is quite rounded.

The carrion crow is a sociable bird, but in the breeding season it is very solitary and maintains its territory. In winter they may form loose flocks but not to the degree of rooks or jackdaws

It inhabits open countryside, usually cultivated with the odd tall tree in which it nests, and it will return to the same nest yearly. Food is varied, carrion principally and in the breeding season it will steal eggs and young.

The crow family has long been considered to be one of the most intelligent group of animals.

The call is a very harsh croak, but they are more silent than the rook.

CHAFFINCH. L 15.5 cm.

Probably our commonest and most widespread finch, with the male particularly an attractive bird. In breeding condition the male has a beautiful blue head, which combined with the white shoulders, wingbar and white outer tail feathers are clear identification features, as is the blue bill. The female also has the white shoulders, wingbars and outer tail feathers, although to a lesser degree. Both sexes have a grey or greenish rump, which splits them from the similar brambling.

Common in woodland, parks, gardens and seem to have a liking for solitary trees in cultivated land. Regular visitor to garden feeders. In winter months will form flocks with other finches and these are seen largely on farmland.

Call is a pleasant trill which usually ends with a terminal flourish. Unlike most birds, this song varies regionally, and keen exponents of bird song claim they can tell from whence the bird came, much like our vocal variances.

In the breeding season they mainly feed on insects, with seeds a large proportion of their winter feed, hence their visits to garden feeders where mine certainly like sunflower hearts.

During the winter months northern European birds visit us in largish flocks, often accompanied by bramblings, adding to our resident population. These arrive in September – October, and depart March – April.

CHIFFCHAFF. L 11cm.

Probably the commonest of our warblers, although it is probably heard more than it is seen. The song is a repeated series of two notes 'silt-salt, silt-salt, silt-salt', these can be easily translated as 'chiff-chaff, chiff-chaff, chiff-chaff' from where the bird gets its name. A few birds over winter but the majority arrive here from mid-March and usually depart between August and October.

Easily confused with its close relative the willow warbler, but that is a more yellowish looking bird. The chiffchaff on the other hand is a drabber and slightly smaller grey-green looking bird with dark legs, and an indistinct supercillium (eyebrow).

Breeds in deciduous and mixed woodlands, with thick undergrowth which is why it is heard more than seen.

We get a passage of birds through the UK from further north as they travel down to their winter grounds. Some of these birds may be the over-wintering birds we have in the UK.

COAL TIT. L 11.5 cm.

The third most common tit you will see on your feeders along with its close relatives, the blue and great tits. The coal tit is the least colourful of the three, with its greyish back, dirty buff underparts, black head and throat patch with white cheeks and a white nape.

It is a restless eater and moves quickly through tops of trees and the outer branches. Its preference is coniferous woodlands and it regularly associates with goldcrests, although it will also be found in mixed woodland and gardens where coniferous trees are present. It does not take to nest boxes as readily as do the blue and great tits, so is not seen so frequently in gardens, and when it is seen it is usually a pair at most.

The young are fed mainly on insects although adult birds also regularly feed on spruce cone seeds, hence their preference for coniferous woodlands.

Northern populations will migrate southwards when food is in short supply.

COLLARED DOVE. L 31 – 33 cm. WS 47 – 55 cm.

A relative newcomer to the British bird list, which prior to the 1940s would have been a very rare bird. Its original home was Asia prior to its spread westwards.

It is now a very common bird seen regularly in parks, gardens, farms, villages and town centres.

They are an attractive slim. long-tailed dove, pale buff with a black band on the neck, unlikely to be confused with any other dove. It is a very active dove and in flight the long tails is a good identification feature when combined with the pale underparts. Juveniles lack the black neck band. Call is a rapid and distinctive 'koo- kooo, koo', oft repeated, which varies from the woodpigeon's 'doo-doooh, doo doo-du'.

It is a tree nesting species, usually preferring isolated trees or hedgerows, coniferous being a particular favourite in built up areas.

They are a resident bird, although some birds do move south in the winter.

COMMON TERN. L 31 -35 cm. WS 82 – 95 cm.

The commonest tern seen inland, just slightly smaller than the Arctic tern with which it is easily confused when seen at distance. The principal differences are the paler undersides and a black tip to the red bill. It is also slightly longer legged and when seen at rest has a flatter forehead with the tail and wing tips ending level with each other.

Although seen round the coast it also breeds frequently far inland by larger lakes and the wetlands near larger rivers. Over recent years it has spread well inland and breeds in many areas in the Midlands, my own county of Staffordshire has several colonies. All our breeding terns are colonial nesting, and if you enter a nesting area you are likely to be subject to attack, and their sharp, pointed bills, are hardy weapons, as I well know.

They are noisy birds especially at their colonies where you will hear the long drawn-out 'kreeer' and a rapid 'kye, kye, kye, kye'. When on normal flight, such as migration, they usually have a short 'kip' call. Feeds on fish.

They are an attractive bird and arrive in the UK April – May and have usually departed between late July and October. Non-breeding birds are likely to leave prior to breeding birds.

COOT. L 36 – 38 cm. WS 70 – 80 cm..

One of our commonest water birds, wherever there is water you are likely to find the coot. They are a sooty black bird with a white bill and frontal plate on the head, and have a bulky build. They establish their breeding territories very early and are aggressive in their defence, and this not only applies to other coots, they will chase birds as large as mallards. Not regularly seen in flight, but when they do take to flight this is in a characteristic tripping run across the surface of the water, accompanied by beating wings. Not very vocal, although they do have a loud, oft repeated 'kowk', if disturbed.

During the winter months they form close-packed flocks which either graze or dive for water plants and small animal matter. A resident in the UK, but many visit us from the continent between October – April.

CORMORANT. L 80 – 100 cm. WS 130 – 16 cm.

A large dark waterbird, with reptilian features. Perches very upright with

22

the wings frequently out-stretched, almost looking as though it was drying the wings.

When in the water it swims low in the water, almost part submerged, with a straight neck and upward tilt to bill. Quite a distinct silhouette. In breeding plumage it has a distinct white patch on rear flanks.

We also see a race of cormorant which visits us from the continent, and this one has much more white on the face and head and a more pronounced white patch on the flanks, and when seen together the differences are quite apparent.

Cormorants were classed as sea birds many years ago, but they are now seen regularly well inland where they now breed in colonies in trees near water, frequently associating with the grey heron. Many never see the sea, nor need it with adequate supplies of fish in freshwater locations. Bird watchers may appreciate the birds, anglers are unlikely to as large numbers would limit fish stocks. Coastal birds are cliff nesting.

CUCKOO. L 32 – 34 cm. WS 55 – 65 cm.

A bird familiar to all by voice, if not recognised by sight. A true sound of summer. They are a long-tailed bird with pointed wings and are regularly confused with kestrels. When seen in flight they usually fly straight and fast with low wing beats, rarely lifting the wings above body level. A very distinctive flight pattern.

Sexes are similar in colour and we have two colour phases, the grey and the red. Well known due to their breeding habits where they lay eggs in other birds' nests and have no further responsibility for the raising of their young.

They are birds of open country with scattered bushes and trees, and open woodland. Here it seeks out the nests of other birds with meadow pipit, dunnock, reed warbler, pied wagtail and redstart being the commonest used. The female apparently chooses just one species whose eggs closely resemble her own.

They commence migration early, the adults leaving from the end of July, with juvenile birds following on late August into September. They return to the UK April – May. Many birds migrate in flocks accompanied by their parents who have travelled the journey before, but the cuckoo, never having known its parents, has to make the journey on its own.

Cuckoos are big insect eaters, especially hairy caterpillars, which are avoided by most birds, and the birds can be seen sitting out on fence posts and the like, seeking out their prey.

An incredible bird, and one we still have much to learn about. One thing we do know, summer would not be summer without the cuckoo.

CURLEW. L 50 – 60 cm. WS 80 – 100 cm.
If it is possible to have a favourite bird, then this is the one. A true bird of wild places with the most evocative call of any bird. To be on a piece of upland moor in the summer, or in an estuary in winter and hear the melodious call 'cour-lee' ringing out, is the true sound of wild places. A call that sends a shiver down your spine.

They are the largest wader living in the UK, where they breed on upland moors, bogs and damp fields and congregate in estuaries during the winter. They are both resident and migrant with birds of passage also moving through. They return to their breeding grounds from March onwards. Females often move off in late June leaving males to look after the young.

In appearance they are a brownish looking bird with a long decurved bill and long legs, which enables them to both wade and feed in deep water. A true wader in every sense of the word. To put it mildly 'some bird' with 'some voice'.

DUNLIN. L 16 – 22 cm. WS 35 – 40 cm.
Probably the commonest wader to be seen during winter along flat shorelines, where many visit us each year, and in several east coast locations they can be seen in their thousands.

They are one of the smallest waders regularly seen, and in summer they are easily recognised by their black belly and brown-red back. In winter they are a greyer looking bird and lose their black underparts and are frequently seen associating with their larger cousin, the knot. At several locations, Snettisham in Norfolk being an example, they and the knot form large flocks and can be seen flighting in their tens of thousands. A wonderful sight at high tide, when they return to land to roost.

In flight they are rarely silent, when they utter a harsh trilled, 'krree', a sound once heard never forgotten. They are both a resident and winter visitor from the far north, Iceland and Scandinavia, and most winters we receive a few of the Greenland race which have crossed the Atlantic to arrive here. In the UK they breed on grassy, boggy moors and lowland marshes, but to be seen in number, winter is the time. Small numbers can be seen inland at lakes and reservoirs.

DUNNOCK. L 14.5 cm.
Commonly known as the hedge sparrow, incorrectly really, as a sparrow it is not. It is a member of the accentor family, and some books still refer to it as the hedge accentor. A regular garden bird where it feeds on insects during the breeding season and seed throughout the remainder of the year.

It is a dark looking little bird, with a thin bill. In the breeding season the male has a grey head, and from the top of a bush will utter a pleasing warble, but only normally heard in the breeding season. A characteristic feature is that the bird frequently runs on the ground with very fluttering wings, giving the impression it is a fussy little bird. It breeds in woodlands with much undergrowth, gardens, parks, scrub and hedgerows particularly in farmland. Not so common in north Scotland.

In the UK it is a resident and very sedentary, rarely moving far from where it was bred, but in the winter months we do receive visitors from northern Europe, mainly September to March/April.

EGYPTIAN GOOSE. L 61 – 73 cm. WS 134 – 154 cm.
An introduced species which has now become widespread, common on many parkland pools and a regular feature on water at many stately homes where it was a collection bird initially. To call it a goose is not strictly correct, it is a large duck species, closely allied with the shelducks. They are principally a ground nesting bird although some will nest in trees. They pair for life.

Although widespread, Norfolk is probably their main breeding location, and here flocks can be very large on several of the nature reserves.

They are a pale brownish bird with large white wing panels and a pronounced dark eye surround. They are a stocky looking bird, with a slightly orange tinge on body, with a dark brown breast patch. The bill is pink-red, darkly outlined, and the long legs are a dull red. Sexes are very similar. In many respects a distinctive looking bird, check on 'Google'.

FIELDFARE. L 25.5 cm.
A common bird in northern Europe, especially Scandinavia and a regular

winter visitor to the UK, where the occasional bird has bred. A distinctive thrush with its grey head, reddish-brown back and arrowhead looking spots on underparts.

In flight shows very pale underside to wings and is usually vocal when in flight when the 'chak, chak, chak' call rings out. Will be found frequently in flocks with other thrushes, redwings especially.

Regularly seen on farmers' fields and short grass areas where they search for worms and the like. They are also big eaters of berries and other fruits and can be seen frequently in gardens feeding on these type of plants. Hawthorn and cotoneaster berries being particular favourites in my garden.

They are often seen in very large flocks, especially in cold weather, and are to be seen in the UK from late September onwards until they depart back north from late March.

GANNET. L 87 – 100 cm. WS 165 – 180 cm.

A powerful looking seabird, long cigar shaped body with long narrow wings. The largest seabird seen regularly around our shores. As an adult bird it is unmistakable, a large white bird with black wing tips (primaries) and in the breeding season the yellowish head is very prominent. They do not reach adult plumage until between 4 – 6 years. Young birds commence with a dark plumage which slowly lightens as they mature.

If any bird can be called a diving bird, then this is it. They perform impressive vertical drives into the water, and these can be from considerable heights. When at sea they are fairly silent, but on their breeding colonies they make loud and grating calls. Colonies can be very large, numbering thousands of birds and are usually on rocky island and steep cliff ledges.

To experience these birds close to hand I suggest you visit the RSPB reserve at Bempton Cliffs in Yorkshire, an amazing place for several species of seabirds. Here gannets fly past just feet away, and their size and powerful flight are easily seen.

They return to their breeding colonies early in the year, but once young can fly they become very much a marine bird and out at sea can be seen flying in a line low over the water. Uncommon inland.

Due to their size were once known as the Solan Goose.

GOLDCREST. L 9cm.

From looking at one of our largest birds, now a chance to look at our smallest bird regularly seen in the UK, being a mere 9 cm in length. You would wonder how a bird this small can survive, let alone migrate to the UK in winter from the continent each year.

Our resident birds frequently visit gardens, but when breeding, prefer coniferous or mixed woodlands especially where spruce are growing. Also regularly seen in churchyards where yew trees grow. It builds an interesting nest, which hangs beneath the twigs like a hammock. During winter regularly seen with mixed flocks of titmice.

The name is very apt. The male has an orange crown stripe, edged black; the female has a yellow crown stripe, also edged black. For a small bird it has a long song, usually referred to as a rising and falling 'seeh sissisyu-see sissisyu-see siss- seeitueet'. I personally have great difficulty in hearing the bird due to the softness of the call.

Although a resident, they are very mobile and our continental visitors are here from September to April.

GOLDFINCH. L 14 cm.

Of all the finches, the goldfinch is probably the most unmistakable, and this applies to both voice and appearance. Rarely silent, their flight call is a soft but rather piercing 'stikelit' or 'stik', once heard easily remembered.

They were a popular cage bird many years ago, especially in the Midlands where they were known as the seven-coloured linnet. An apt description.

Since we commenced to feed birds in our gardens regularly they have become a common garden species, and in consequence their numbers have increased greatly.

They are now probably the commonest finch seen in most gardens. Can be seen in spring and summer on open cultivated fields with copses, wooded areas and hedgerows. The young are fed on insects but adult birds are big seed eaters. Their rather pointed bill is ideal for extracting seeds from thistles, burdocks and teasels, and as garden bird feeders know only too well, from seed containers. Here they can be very argumentative and fights occur regularly, not too seriously I am pleased to say.

Their red, white and black faces, combined with their distinctive black and yellow wings, make them easily recognisable. They also have a white rump.

All the goldfinches you see are not resident birds. Many British breeding birds move south in the winter, as far as the western Mediterranean, this occurs during September to October, returning home March – April, and northern European birds pass through the UK during October – November and return through March – April.

GREAT BLACK-BACKED GULL. L 64 – 78 cm. WS 150 – 170 cm.
The largest of our native gulls and a west coast species principally. Not very common inland where our other two larger gulls, the herring and lesser-black backed, outnumber it.

It is a broad winged gull, back darker than the lesser black-backed gull and heavy billed. When perched the large white wing tips are always visible and the longish legs are a grey-pink. Breeds commonly on rocky coasts, where they are at times solitary birds, although local flocks are to be found.

A very aggressive bird, not one to be argued with. They eat fish, eggs, young birds, carrion and will kill a full-grown duck, and are capable of making a kill on land, sea or in the air. Great black-backed gulls also chase other gulls and terns making them disgorge their food, and will catch slower flying birds such as puffins on the wing.

All gulls will defend their nests against all comers, man included, and to have one attack you is far from pleasant, believe me, I know. A bird to study from a distance.

They take 3 to 4 years to mature and are largely a resident species.

GREAT CRESTED GREBE. L 46 – 51 cm. WS 85 – 90 cm.
Our largest and commonest grebe, which in its summer plumage is unmistakable with its brownish-red and black head plumes which stand out like a ruff, tippets as they are known. It has a long white neck and a white face. In winter it loses the bold head colours and becomes a whiter looking bird with a dark crown.

Many years ago the bird was killed for these tippets which were used in ladie's hat manufacturing, and a society was formed to protect the bird and stop this killing, the forerunner of the RSPB Queen Victoria also became involved in this and it is claimed she barred anyone coming to court wearing these feathers.

In flight they are very characteristic, very elongated and have rapid, whirring wingbeats, a flight style typical of all the grebes. In the breeding season the birds perform many displays; they float almost breast to breast, tippets raised with much head-waggling and mock preening, at times almost looking like they are walking on water.

They build an unusual nest. This is usually on a platform, which is then attached to vegetation and as water levels rise, the nest is capable of also rising, saving nests from being flooded. They are to be found on shallow lakes and ponds in the breeding season, and in winter they will move onto larger stretches of water such as reservoirs, bigger lakes and sheltered sea bays, where large flocks may be seen.

Although principally a resident bird, many northern breeding birds do move south for the winter. Feeds on fish and smaller aquatic animals and when at sea will take shrimps.

They are not a very vocal bird apart from in the spring when they utter various grating calls and when displaying they will utter an heron-like 'aoor' and an oft repeated 'kek, kek, kek'.

A bird to grace any stretch of water, especially when in full plumage.

GREAT SPOTTED WOODPECKER. L 22 – 23 cm. WS 34 – 39 cm.
The commonest of our woodpeckers, and the one most likely to come into people's gardens where birds are regularly fed. Here it has a love of peanuts.

It is basically a black, white and red bird. The male has a red nape with red belly, and the white breast has a pinkish tint. The female is similar but lacks the red nape. They are probably heard more often than seen, when a metallic 'kuk' or 'kik' is heard, and if irritated these calls are repeated as a rapid chatter. Its drumming is the fastest of all the woodpeckers and consists of between 10 and 15 strikes per second.

The sound travels some distance. It drums on dead branches and trunks, and occasionally will attack telegraph poles. There have even been reports of it drumming on metal chimneys and the like. Feeds on insects, their larvae, eggs and young birds and the seeds of trees, especially conifers where it attacks the cones to obtain the seeds.

Northern birds which feed on spruce and pine cones can erupt in years when there is a shortage of these, otherwise, they are normally sedentary, not moving far from where they breed.

Although a true woodland species they are regularly seen in parks and gardens.

GREAT TIT. L 14cm.

One of the commonest of woodland birds and a frequent garden visitor, especially where food is made available. Will regularly breed in gardens where nest boxes are provided, and although a woodland species is rarely seen in pure coniferous woodland. Here it nests in holes, natural or created by other birds, woodpeckers for instance.

Probably the most boldly coloured of our titmice, and certainly the largest.

Sexes are similar, having yellow underparts with a black central band (frequently referred to as its waistcoat), glossy black head with large white cheek patches with a moss green back, and white wing bars on the blue-grey wings. The female has a narrower central black band and the yellow underparts are slightly paler.

Has quite a varied range of calls, but two in particular are regularly heard, a cheery 'tse weeda weet' or 'pink tche-che-che' will ring out. They will commence calling as early as January on sunny days.

Mainly a resident species, but on occasion will erupt from northern and eastern Europe, at times in large numbers.

GREENFINCH. L 15 cm.

The largest of our yellow-green finches, powerfully billed and a muscular looking bird. Very argumentative and usually the top bird at feeding stations, where they will tackle birds larger them themselves. I have regularly seen them chase starlings off.

In the breeding season the colour of the bird becomes more striking and the yellow markings on the wings and tail become more noticeable, especially when seen in flight.

Among its various calls the male announces his presence with an oft repeated wheezing 'dchweeesh', instantly recognisable when once heard. They also have a very mellow and rich song which is quite canary-like. It also performs a song flight with slow wingbeats, which is quite distinctive.

A bird of open country, city parks, gardens, hedgerows and farmland where it feeds on various seeds, and comes to bird tables frequently, especially during the winter, where hemp and sunflower hearts are particular favourites.

As with most of our finches, they are a resident species with winter visitors from the continent, seen during October to April.

GREY HERON. L 90 – 98 cm. WS 150 – 175 cm.

The most common of the heron species to be seen in the UK, although in recent years this is being challenged by the little egret, but more of that later.

They are a colonial nesting species, building their nests in trees, frequently now along with cormorants. You may on occasion find a single pair nesting, then it is likely to be in a reed bed, not in a tree.

Non birders frequently think they have seen a stork in flight when they have seen a heron. The heron family fly with their necks tucked in, storks have their necks extended fully.

The heron in colour is basically a grey, black and white bird; in the breeding season it has an extended black crest on the head. It is powerfully billed, adults having yellowish bills; the juveniles have a darker bill and lack the crest.

Despite being a large bird, they are frequently overlooked as they stand, motionless, waiting for their prey to swim by. They are big fish eaters but will also feed on small animals and insects, and are regularly seen standing alone in fields waiting for insects to appear. They also visit garden ponds where fish are bred, as happened with me many years ago.

Although being colonial nesting, they disperse from their colonies in the late summer to seek out fish-rich waters. They return to their colonies very early in the year and are one of our earliest breeding species.

Although being a residential species, we do get occasional visitors from the continent during the winter months.

GREYLAG GOOSE. L 75 – 90 cm. WS 147 – 180 cm.

Aptly named being a uniform brown-grey looking bird, with a quite large orange bill, and pink legs, and after the Canada our commonest goose breeding in the UK. In flight they have a striking silver-grey panel on the wings, hence the name.

Our breeding species, especially in England and Wales, are mainly feral, descendents from home bred birds for shooting purposes and collections. True wild greylags are either winter visitors from the far north, Iceland in particular, or birds breeding in the far north of the UK.

If it was not for Canada and greylag geese, we would not see many geese during the summer months, as the majority of geese seen are winter visitors from further north, and we receive many thousands of these each winter.

Geese are rarely seen singularly, they are very much a flock bird, and greylags are no different. Common now on many a park pool where they can at times outnumber the resident Canada geese. Here they are a very noisy goose, sounding very like the domestic goose, which probably originated from the greylag in the first instance.

They are a very heavy bird and in flight look very big headed and thick necked, and are the largest of the grey geese to be seen in the UK.

GREY WAGTAIL. L 18 – 19 cm.

To my mind this is the most attractive of the wagtails we see in the UK, and is the longest tailed of them. We are lucky in the fact it is a resident and can be seen all year, whereas the yellow wagtail, with which it gets confused, is only here in the summer.

The male bird especially, has a black throat, grey back and head with the complete underside a bright yellow, and dark brownish black wings, with a white wingbar, a striking combination of colours. On the female the colours are more subdued with a white belly and white throat, still attractive nevertheless.

During the breeding season is seen frequently by running water; in winter will visit lakes, the coast and in the south a regular sighting on watercress beds.

It is a very lively bird, catching insects both in the air and on the ground, and is seen running rapidly after these at speed.

Although a resident there is much movement with birds moving down from upland areas to lowland areas during the winter.

GUILLEMOT. L 38 – 45 cm. WS 64 – 73 cm.

A member of the auk family, and only seen on land during the breeding season. A true seabird in every sense of the word, frequently confused with the razorbill where they differ in shape of bill and have paler upperparts.

They are a cliff nesting species on sea facing cliffs, and these colonies can be very large. Very noisy on their breeding sites where high growling 'arrr' and ooarr' calls are heard. Another bird you would not want to be nesting in your own garden!

At these colonies an interesting variant of the guillemot can be seen, the 'bridled' version. This bird has a white eye–ring and a white line beyond the eye, almost looking as though it was wearing a pair of spectacles. It is not a different bird, just a variant.

Auks are great swimmers, and the guillemot is no exception; they can dive deeply and their constant food is fish. They arrive at their breeding locations in January and have normally departed by August. They breed on open ledges with nests very close to each other where constant bickering takes place. They make little or no nest and their eggs are very pointed at one end which helps to stop them falling off the ledge whenever the sitting bird departs. The shape helps the egg to spin and stay in position.

HERRING GULL. L 55 – 67 cm. WS 130 – 158 cm.

Probably the commonest gull seen on our coast, where its deep-voiced 'aoou' is a constant sound to any seaside holiday. With visitors feeding the gulls so often, in some seaside holiday resorts they have become a nuisance, and at times have been known to injure people by flying at them to steal ice creams and the like. Feeding them is now an offence.

An adult herring gull is a very smart and clean looking bird with grey back and wings which have black tips, brilliant white plumage, striking yellow eyes and pink legs; it is some bird. They do not attain their adult plumage until their fourth year, juveniles looking a very dark grey. They have a close relative, the yellow-legged gull, which has yellow legs not pink. So it pays to look closely at the herring gull as yellow-legged are being seen more often. This bird has spread from western Europe in recent years.

Back to our bird. It is common on coasts, and larger lakes, sometimes well inland, and nests on islands and cliffs. Feeds on fish, fish offal, eggs, young birds, carrion and refuse; regularly seen on refuse tips where it sorts out discarded food, plus anything we care to give it. Will also chase down migrating birds coming in over the sea.

An aggressive bird, not one to get too close to.

HOUSE MARTIN. L 12.5 cm.

A common summer migrant which is well associated with man as it nests colonially on buildings. Not only buildings, also on cliff faces frequently on the coast.

Along with the swallow and cuckoo, a true herald of summer.

33

Arriving back here April/May and departing August/October, with a few reports of birds overwintering in the UK. Their mud made nests regularly seen on buildings even in well built up areas.

Seen over open water as they hunt for flying insects. Frequently confused with the swallow, but the lack of long tail streamers and combined with having a white rump, it's usually enough to separate the two. Where the two are seen in quantity, the house martin usually feeds at a slightly higher altitude than the swallow, and does not sweep low over the water to quite the same extent as swallows do. With the lack of tail streamers it is also a much smaller bird.

Frequently seen perched on telephone wires where it sings. A pleasant babbling twitter, very much a sound of summer, I always feel, almost a conversational sound.

Now frequently referred to as the common house martin.

HOUSE SPARROW. L 15 cm.

One of commonest birds, very much associated with man, be that in built up areas or farmyards. In recent years there has been a decline in numbers due to modern building methods which has meant they are finding less suitable nesting sites.

We can do much to redress this by providing nest boxes for their use. They are one of the most well known of birds and grace many a city centre, be a tragedy if we lost it.

Male instantly recognised by the brown crown, black bib, and a dark brown band from the eye backwards across the nape. The female is a nondescript grey-buff. Both sexes have a pale wing bar, almost white in the male.

They are frequently described as chatty birds, and they do have a monotonous 'chip, chip', 'chap, chap', or 'cheerp', and when heard in a flock this can be deafening. In flight they have a 'tweet, tweet' call.

Their principal food is mostly seeds and insects, but will readily take food provided by us, and consequently are regular visitors to feeding stations.

Nests in holes, usually beneath roof tiles and boxes. Occasionally you will find them nesting in a bush where they build a large roofed nest with a side entrance. A very well built construction.

They are a resident found in most part of the country where man lives.

JACKDAW. L 33 cm.

The smallest member of the crow family breeding in the UK, common and widespread. As with all crows, a very intelligent bird as I know from having one as a pet many years ago.

It is a uniform black bird with a grey nape and a pale eye. They are a very agile flier that frequently soars. Flocks can be seen carrying out almost acrobatic manoeuvres where they use the air currents. They communally roost and are regularly seen along with rooks, they will even nest alongside rooks.

Breeds colonially in towns, cities, frequently in older parks, on church towers, other older buildings and cliffs. Also a woodland species and in rows of trees where nest holes are available. With many houses now centrally heated and no open fires, the frequently nest in house chimneys, here as solitary pairs.

They are regular visitors to gardens where they will feed on scraps and seed put out for the birds. Common on fields and farmland where they seek out insects and worms.

Their commonest call, frequently heard in flight, is a metallic sounding 'kya' or 'chak'. Unmistakable, almost as though it is calling out its own name.

It is a resident, quite sedentary, although some do migrate from northern Europe, and they pair for life.

JAY. L 34 cm.

Slightly larger than the jackdaw and the most colourful of the crow family, having conspicuous white and pale blue wing patches, combined with a bold white rump, noticeable when in flight.

They are a shy but common woodland species, where they are noticed more by their call, a noisy and far-carrying 'kraih'. Autumn is a good time to see this bird, especially if you have any oak trees growing locally. They regularly commute to these to collect up acorns for the winter, which they will bury for the future. Many a mighty oak probably needs to thank a jay. Best seen when they are in a gliding flight when their colours show well.

Breeds in both deciduous and coniferous woodlands where it favours areas of young spruce or pine, but can be seen in parks and suburban areas with many trees.

Feeds on insects, tree fruits, eggs and the young of smaller birds. Will visit garden feeders, but usually these gardens are large and have sheltering trees.

They are a resident species, but in some years we have visitors cross from northern Europe.

A bird to both look out for and listen in to when on your woodland walks.

KESTREL. L 33 – 39 cm. WS 65 – 80 cm.
Frequently seen hovering and perched on roadside posts and wires where its long tail silhouette is distinctive. At one time it was considered to be our most common bird of prey, but in recent years it may well have been taken over by the buzzard.

Sexes can be confused when seen at distance, but the male has a grey head and tail, with a black tip; the female lacks the grey head and has a barred tail.

When seen and heard round their nest sights, they are very noisy where they will utter a piercing 'kee kee kee kee', which can be heard at some distance.

Regular haunts being cultivated fields, heaths, meadows, moorland, and bogs up as high as the willow zone in mountainous country. Breeds in holes, old crows' nests, cliffs and in towns on ledges, where it is quite common.

Feeds on rodents, smaller birds usually taken from the ground, frogs and larger insects. It is mainly a resident in the UK, with winter visitors from northern Europe.

KINGFISHER. L 16 – 17cm. WS 24 – 26 cm.
People frequently say to me that we do not have any really colourful birds. To those I usually say, have a look at a kingfisher, it rivals any bird in the world. Just 'Google' it, and I think you will agree with me. Unfortunately, for casual observers, the bird is not often seen. It is more noticed from its penetrating loud 'zeeeee' or 'sreeee' as it flashes past with its back flashing a brilliant turquoise-blue. In flight it is very fast and low over the water, with whirring wing beats and brief glides.

It frequently sits out on branches, low over the water, where it searches for food beneath, and once seen it dives, beak first, into the water. For such a colourful bird it merges in well with the leaf colour of its chosen perch. More often seen on clear flowing rivers and streams where it has good banks in which to dig out a tunnel up to a metre long, in which to nest. Also seen on ponds and deep ditches.

Feeds on fish, aquatic insects and other smaller animals found in water. In the winter many move to the coast and larger inland waters.

KITTIWAKE. L 38 – 40 cm. WS 95 – 108 cm.
Probably our commonest gull, which breeds in very large colonies on steep cliffs in many parts of the country, and occasionally found breeding on tall coastal buildings.

A very neat and tidy gull, yellow billed, jet black eye, grey mantle and upper wings, jet black wing tips and black legs, head, breast and underparts brilliant white.

For such an attractive bird, it is a pity we cannot say the same thing about its voice.

They are the noisiest of gulls at the nesting site, where the shrill, rather nasal 'kevi-week' echoes round the cliff face. Almost as though they were shouting out their name. You would not want them nesting at the bottom of your garden, that is for sure.

The most marine of all our gulls. After breeding they spend their time out at sea, in the North Sea and Atlantic, and mainly seen from land during passage and in westerly storms, usually during spring and autumn. Very occasionally seen inland.

They feed on small marine animals, fish and offal, the majority of which is taken from the water, rarely seen feeding on dry ground unlike other gulls.

KNOT. L 23 – 25 cm. WS 47 – 54 cm.
Possibly the commonest wader seen in the UK, although they rarely breed here. We receive vast numbers each winter which have migrated down ·from the near Arctic to spend the winter in our many estuaries and coastal marshlands. Here their vast flocks perform spectacularly as they fly in from incoming tides.

In their summer plumage they have a reddish breast and face, but we rarely see them in this condition. Ours are invariably juvenile birds or adults in winter plumage, when they are a greyish looking bird with greenish legs. In flight they have a narrow white wingbar and a pale grey rump. Their bill is black and straight and legs are greenish-grey.

Not only do we have large numbers visit us each winter, we also have birds on passage which migrate as far south as west Africa. Although predominantly a coastal bird, can be seen on shores of lakes and reservoirs inland, but only in small numbers.

To really enjoy them, the coast is the place, and the muddier the better.

Flocks of birds have been given differing names by birders, and flocks of waders are regularly referred to as 'a Confusion'. Confusing to us it may be, it certainly is not to them, they are fully aware of what they are doing. To see birds in such numbers and behaving so, is one of nature's wonders.

LAPWING. L 28 – 31 cm. WS 70 – 76 cm.
The one wading bird most easily recognised. A characteristic bird on coastal pastures and farmland is how I saw it once described, and I can put it no better. In my early days we referred to it as the 'peewit' due to its shrill 'peoo-wit' call, and it was much commoner then. Very much a bird of farmland. It is now a less common bird and is giving concern about its future, now we see it much more frequently in winter.

In appearance it stands out amongst our other common waders. The long wispy crest and greenish back, combined wth a general appearance of it being a black and white looking bird, makes identification simple. Due to the greenish back, the bird was also known as the green plover many years ago. A most distinctive and attractive bird.

It is found on fields and meadowland with short grasses and slightly damp areas, especially where next to wetlands. In winter it flocks up, a deceit as it is known, and when in flight is very graceful and performs many acrobatics; if ever a bird looked as though it was flying just for fun, the lapwing is it. If you are close enough to a flock you can hear a humming from its wings.

It is a resident, winter visitor and a bird of passage to breeding ground further north, and feeds on ground invertebrates, insects, worms etc.

It is a bird I grew to love when young, and that feeling has remained throughout my life. Long live the 'peewit'.

LESSER BLACK-BACKED GULL. L 52 – 67 cm. WS 128 – 148 cm.

Slightly smaller than the great black-backed gull and has yellow legs and a smaller bill. We see two races in the UK. The western European race is more a slate-grey above and the Baltic race is much darker, almost resembling the great black-backed in colour, but not in size. We see both in the UK.

As a breeding bird they are more coastal, where they breed in loose colonies, although in recent years they have moved inland and breed in many cities, using the flat roofs of tower blocks as their breeding locations. The next best thing to a cliff from a bird's point of view.

As with most of the larger gulls, they are very piratical and will attack smaller species to make them disgorge their food. Walking through a colony of lesser black- backs is not recommended.

They are the commonest of the larger gulls to be seen inland where they frequent large lakes and reservoirs, and feed on open fields, especially during the winter.

LINNET. L 14 cm.

Widespread in the UK apart from the mountainous areas of Scotland. A bird frequently overlooked, sexes similar except in the breeding season when the male has a more intense pinkish-buff tone to chest. In flight quite distinctive when the brown back and pale wing flashes are seen.

They are a superb song bird and were regularly kept as captive birds many years ago. The song is best described as very melodious, with indrawn twittering, whirring sequences and fluted notes woven together. "I thank Lars Jonsson for that apt description."

Linnets are associated mainly with open ground with a spread of bushes, especially gorse and thorn, and young plantations with cover, in the winter on fields, rough ground and marshes where flocks will form.

They are a resident in the UK, although they will move from their breeding territories in the winter when they form into their flocks, and we also get winter visitors from northern Europe which arrive September – October and depart March – April. A bird most definitely worth listening out for.

LITTLE EGRET. L 55 – 65 cm. WS 88 – 95 cm.

The commonest white heron to be seen in the UK. Until late 1900s this was a very rare bird in the UK, and I well remember journeying up to

Anglesey to see my first one in the UK. I need not have bothered, I have now seen them flying over my own garden, they are so common and widespread. In some areas they outnumber the grey heron.

Unmistakable in appearance, being a brilliant white with a contrasting long black bill, black legs and distinctive yellow feet, easily seen when in flight, which avoids confusion with the all white cattle egret. In the breeding season they have distinctive long nape plumes.

Colonial nesting, now frequently sharing these with grey herons so the two are seen close together.

Normally seen in or near to water: shallow lakes, rivers, ponds and also marshy areas and lagoons on the coast. Principal food is fish, although they will take any small water creature, and do feed on damp ground were worms and the like are taken.

They are now a resident bird in the UK, although we may still get occasional migrants.

LITTLE GREBE. L 25 – 29 cm. WS 40 – 45 cm.
A small dumpy and dark looking grebe, with a bright yellow gape to bill, quite distinctive on adult birds in summer plumage. In winter is a much paler bird showing white on neck and lower back.

It breeds on well vegetated ponds and rivers where it can be difficult to see due to its secretive behaviour. More often heard than seen, when the bubbling like call which is not unlike that of a female cuckoo, lets you know the bird is in attendance.

When seen on open water dives frequently where it feeds on water insects, small fish and molluscs.

Best seen in winter when they appear on open water, lakes, reservoirs, open bays and similar. Not usually in great numbers, just a few, unlike the great crested grebe which can be seen in large flocks during winter.

A resident bird in the UK with numbers visiting us from northern Europe in the winter.

LITTLE OWL. L 21 – 23 cm. WS 50 – 56 cm.
The smallest owl regularly seen in the UK. Probably the commonest owl seen in England and Wales, not widespread in Scotland. They are not a native species and were introduced to the UK from the continent, and quickly became established.

They are the most diurnal of the owls and can frequently be seen as a brown-grey lump sitting out on telegraph poles, open rock, barn roofs and fences, usually at dusk. If disturbed when roosting, rarely flies far away, and in defence of their nests they are very aggressive for their size. When agitated by another bird they stand more upright and bob about almost like a robin. In flight, flies in deep undulations with folded wings in glides, rarely any great distance apart from when hunting.

During the breeding season the usual call heard is a drawn out 'koooah', with an occasional shorter and more piercing 'kiU'.

Occurs in open cultivated areas, frequently near to large gardens, avenues of trees and various buildings where suitable holes for nesting are provided. Food consists of small rodents, small birds, insects, worms and snails.

LONG-TAILED TIT. L 12 – 14 cm.

One of the smallest birds in body size in the UK, more tail than body. I once read it described as a fluffy ball of wool with a long tail. I could not have put it better myself. It looks basically a black and white bird, although it is more subtle than that.

It flocks up in winter with other titmice, and it is instantly recognised by its shape and rather piercing call 'tsee, tsee, tsee', and the habit of flying after each other rather than in loose flocks.

They are found in deciduous woodlands, open terrain with bushes and hedgerows in the summer, and occasionally nesting in large gardens. They build a rather elaborate nest covered in lichens with an oval side entrance. They also keep together as a family group throughout the autumn and winter, although they too join in with other flocks of titmice. Feed mostly on spiders and small insects, although in recent years have also taken to bird feeders, so have become a regular winter garden bird.

Long-tailed tits are mainly sedentary but roam locally during the winter, frequently joining in loose titmice flocks.

A delightful little bird which I remember as a flying lollipop.

Of our titmice species, the only member which does not use holes for breeding purposes, unlike the blue, great, coal, marsh and willow tit.

MAGPIE. L 44 – 48cm.

The most readily recognised member of the crow family. An elegant black and white, long tailed bird, and of all the crows, the one more closely associated with man and a regular garden visitor. One of the few crows to have a nursery rhyme about it.

'One is for sorrow, two for joy', and this rhyme dates back two to three hundred years, which gives you a good indication of how long the bird has been associated with man.

This is the commonest crow in built-up areas, builds its nest in trees, which is a large oval nest of sticks with a large size entrance, easily seen in winter when the trees and bushes are without leaf. They pair for life which is where the 'two for joy' line comes in. The young, when they have been driven off by their adults and lack territories of their own, often gather in flocks and roost communally.

They have wide appetites' and their food includes eggs and young of other species which they take from the nests, large insects, carrion and any food we put out for them. Truly omnivorous.

The expression 'thieving magpie' comes from their love of bright things; their nests are frequently decorated with bright objects such as silver paper etc.

MALLARD. L 51 – 62 cm. WS 81 – 98 cm.

Once known as the wild duck, a bird fed by many a child when visiting a park pool. The first bird I learned the name of, and it became my introduction to the bird world.

The drake is a superbly coloured bird, unlike the female, although both sport the blue wing panel. With the majority of the dabbling ducks it is the drake which is colourful, the females are generally drab, good camouflage when sitting on the nest.

Drake ducks go into what is known as 'eclipse plumage' after breeding, and this is very similar to the plumage of the female, and can at times make sexing the bird rather difficult. With the mallard however, voice is a good guide. Only the female 'quacks'; the drake's call is a rather nasal 'vaehp'. Also the drake maintains its yellowish bill; the female's bill is much darker.

In the breeding season they are found on freshwater locations, lakes, ponds, rivers, streams etc. We also get migrants from northern Europe during the winter, so the mallard on your park pool may not be one of ours. At certain waters the winter flocks can be substantial.

Their food is very variable, seeds, plants, fruits, insects and other small aquatic creatures, plus for some, food provided by us. Will also be seen feeding on damp pastures and fields.

Our commonest and most well known duck.

MARSH TIT. L 11.5 cm.
Easily confused with the willow tit. Has a glossy black cap and smaller black bib when compared to the willow tit. The wing colouring is uniform, lacking the pale wing panel of the willow tit. Voice is the clearest identification feature. It has an almost explosive 'pitchou' call and a repeated chirpy whistle 'chiu, chiu, chiu' and a rather grating 'psiche-che-che-che-che-che'. These calls ring out clearly, so you are likely to hear the bird more frequently than see it.

They are birds of deciduous or mixed woods, often near to streams or lakeshores, parkland and large gardens. Feeds on seeds, insects and during the winter months comes into smaller gardens where seed is made available.

Marsh tits are resident and in the main very sedentary.

MEADOW PIPIT. L 14.5 cm.
The commonest of the pipits seen in the UK, having a distinctly streaked mantle and rump. Common in open meadowland, shore meadows, boggy areas and heathland, with the upland moors being a particular favourite area during the breeding season.

At times may be confused with the skylark by the inexperienced bird watcher, as it sings on the wing, especially when rising, then slowly descending, but will also sing when perched on the top of a bush or post. Not with quite the quality of a skylark however.

During the winter will flock up and then is regularly seen on lake shores. In the UK the bird is both a resident and summer migrant, but the larger numbers are usually seen in the winter when our birds are bolstered up by migrants from northern Europe.

MISTLE THRUSH. L 27 cm.
Our largest resident thrush, a heavy and long-tailed looking bird. Similarly marked as the song thrush, but has a pronounced grey appearance and a white tip to outer tail feathers which is visible when the bird lands. Flight is very undulating and it closes its wings similarly to a woodpigeon.

Frequently calls when in flight, a harsh rattling 'rrrr' announces its presence, and the song is similar to that of the song thrush, but is more fluty with well-marked pauses between the notes. You will regularly hear the bird singing in poor weather conditions when other birds are silent, hence it being also known as the 'stormcock'.

It is one of our earliest breeding species and breeds in larger gardens, parks, woods and orchards, and some have a decided preference for conifer plantations.

Feeds on worms, snails, insects, fruit and berries, with the name mistle coming from the fact it eats mistletoe berries, and because of this it is believed the bird helps the mistletoe to spread.

The majority of our birds are residents with just a small number migrating from the continent each winter

MOORHEN. L 32 – 35 cm. WS 50 – 55 cm

Unmistakable, and one of our commonest water birds. When swimming shows its characteristic white tail with constant tail jerks. A uniformly rich brown bird with flashes of white on the sides, with a bold yellow and red bill. Legs and feet are green, and although it is a water bird the feet are not webbed, they are lobed.

It has many calls and will sing at night when a persistent 'kreck-kreck-kreck' can be heard.

During the breeding season is less frequently seen as it nests in reedbeds, river banks, ponds where there is sheltered vegetation of reeds, bulrushes and willows.

It has a varied diet of plants, seeds, fruits, insects and small animals. Will readily come for food on park pools where they are frequently seen.

Mainly a resident in the UK with just a few winter visitors from Scandinavia and the Low Countries.

MUTE SWAN. L 145 – 160 cm. WS 208 – 238 cm.

The largest bird regularly breeding in the UK, and a most familiar bird on any park pool, lakes, reservoirs and rivers. On park pools appears almost tame, coming up for food and can be quite aggressive in seeking it. Needs no description, differs from our other two wild swans, the Bewick's and whooper swans by the graceful curve in the neck and the reddish bill with the black knob. Also, it is a resident, whereas the two mentioned above are winter visitors. Young mute swans, cygnets, are brownish and take a year to obtain their white plumage.

Apart from when showing anger, they are a silent bird, hence their name, and in flight their wings produce a throbbing whine, which make identification when in flight, easier. The wing beats of the whooper swan for instance, are almost silent, they announce their presence by voice.

They pair for life and build a large nest made of reeds and similar. They usually do not breed until they are three years old, and have been recorded to live for 15 years or more.

Feed on aquatic plants which are grazed from the bottom in shallow water.

They regularly form into large flocks, in both the summer and winter, the summer flocks usually being non breeding birds. Winter flocks can also be seen on sea coasts and in estuaries.

NUTHATCH. L 14 cm.

A very active and chirpy woodland species. Constantly on the move, or so it seems, and is one of the few birds which can both climb and descend trees head first, as well as walk on the undersides of branches. It is a true woodland species, although they are becoming a more regular visitor to gardens.

Due to their colour I frequently refer to them as the kingfisher of the woods.

They appear almost neckless at times, with a big head and for the size of the bird, a long pointed bill. They are a blue-grey on upper surfaces with a rusty-buff breast and belly, and on the head they have a distinct black eye line. A colourful bird.

They frequent deciduous woodlands, especially those with mature oak trees, and when the trees are in full foliage their voice is the best way of identifying them. This is a penetrating 'peeu, peeu, peeu' that really does ring out. They feed on spiders, insects, nuts and seeds, and during the winter months will regularly visit garden bird tables seeking food. Here you will see them take a peanut to a suitable perch where they will hammer it to pieces, using their bill like a chisel.

They use existing holes for their nest, and the bird places mud round the entrance of the hole to bring it down to the required size.

Nuthatch are residents in the UK and in the winter months they can be seen attached to titmice flocks.

OSPREY. L 55 – 69 cm. WS 145 – 160 cm.

In flight the bird has a distinctive black and white appearance, with long narrow wings, which unlike the majority of the larger birds of prey, usually only four primaries (fingers) are visible, as against them showing five or six. Although looking black and white at distance, their wings and upper parts are a grey-brown.

They were once lost as a breeding bird in the UK, but in the last sixty years or so they have staged a recovery. From the first pair which bred in Scotland at Loch Garten, they have spread to other areas including England. Away from breeding locations they are normally a bird of passage, on transit to or from their breeding sites, and in spring and autumn can be seen at many large lakes and reservoirs, where they may stay for a few days, providing wonderful views.

At times as they glide or circle over water they can be easily confused with an immature great black-backed gull, but once it sights suitable prey it descends in stages, legs dangling, then dives at speed into the water. With the speed and power of the dive they often completely disappear beneath the surface. They will also hover prior to the final dive.

They nest in trees and on cliffs where they build their nests, which are used for many years and in consequence can become very large structures.

Ospreys are a summer migrant, arriving April – May and return to their winter grounds in Africa and the western Mediterranean, September onwards.

OYSTERCATCHER. L 40 – 45 cm. WS 80 – 86 cm.

No mistaking this bird by voice or appearance. It is a striking black and white bird with a powerful long red bill, and is very noisy, especially where nesting. You will hear the high pitched 'kubeek. kubeek' or 'pik, pik' ring out should you approach near to their nesting site, and this call no doubts informs any other bird nesting locally that a predator is about. In flight they show a very broad white wing bar, which is not visible when standing still.

Males frequently gather together where they walk around bent down, uttering various calls and long drawn out trills. Looking almost as though they are dancing.

Although mainly seen as a coastal bird, many breed far inland; most reservoirs have a pair or two in attendance. As their name indicates, they feed on cockles, mussels, crustaceans, with inland species supplementing their diet with worms and insects.

Although a resident in the UK, we do get partial migrants, birds on passage and winter visitors.

PHEASANT. L 53 – 89 cm male, female L 53 – 66 cm. WS 70 – 90 cm.
Was first introduced into eastern Europe as many as 2,000 years ago from Asia, and into northern Europe about 200 years ago, so it is a relatively new species in the UK. It is probably the commonest game bird we have, with many thousands being bred and released each year for shooting.

Cock birds vary in appearance depending upon from which race they originated. The common race, which shows the white neck-ring, is the Chinese variant. A cock pheasant is probably one of our most colourful birds, and no description is really necessary. The female is equally quickly identified due to her long tail.

A common bird of cultivated country, with small areas of woodland, clumps of trees and hedgerows, where they are regularly seen in groups. In flight, which they do infrequently, preferring to run away from danger, their wings make a loud whirring noise. Not the most graceful of fliers.

Food is very varied, and includes vegetable matter, seeds, fruits, nuts, roots and plants, with the chicks also taking insects and other small animals. In recent times has commenced to visit feeding stations and can be seen in gardens, especially large gardens.

PIED WAGTAIL. L 18 cm.
In Europe we have two races of this bird, the nominate species, the white wagtail, and in the UK the race, our pied wagtail. Our bird is very much a black and white bird, whereas the continental bird has a grey back. When studying pied wagtails it always pays to look at them closely, as a few white wagtails do visit us annually.

The pied wagtail is a common and widespread bird in the UK, found in most habitats with open sunlit areas where insects collect, be this town or country, familiar on most city car parks, especially where surface water lies attracting insects.

Nests on buildings, especially where near to water, bridges and river banks, and is a big insect eater. It will pursue these quite energetically and

47

in recent years has become a frequent visitor to garden feeders. Here it is to be seen feeding on the dropped seed.

Obviously a resident bird with a few crossing over to the near continental coast and because of the association with water was known as the water wagtail.

PUFFIN. L 26 – 29 cm. WS 47 – 63 cm

Probably the most well known British bird, although seen by few people. A true bird of the sea, only seen on land when breeding. We are all familiar with the bird's brightly coloured bill, which contrasts with its black and white plumage.

This only has colour in the breeding season, the remainder of the year the bill is smaller and becomes a predominantly yellow and grey bill.

They are a coastal cliff breeding species, where they excavate burrows in the grassy slopes and will also use rabbit burrows. They nest at times in very large colonies and are rarely found on their own. Once the young have left their nest they quickly move well out to sea, and apart from strong gales are unlikely to return to land until they are ready to breed.

Their breeding colonies are spread around the coast wherever steep cliffs are available, but are more frequent the further north you go. Due to climate change there is a real worry that both Wales and England could lose this bird as a breeding species due to sea temperatures rising. Sand eels are a large part of their diet whilst breeding, and as the sea temperature rises these are slowly moving further north so the puffin could soon only be found in Scotland. That would be a tragedy.

RAVEN. L 65 cm.

Our largest passerine and member of the crow family, considerably larger than its cousin the carrion crow, who it rivals as our only other completely black species.

Easily identified by size and when in flight by the wedge shaped tail and heavy head and bill. Frequently soars on flattened wings and can be confused as a bird of prey, but when it calls, no confusion. It has a far-carrying, deep and metallic 'krrooap, krrooap,' a sound which really suits the bird.

In recent years they have spread to many parts of the country, following the buzzard and are a common sight. It is not that many years ago I used to visit Wales in the hope of seeing this majestic bird, now they come to visit me, and I live in Staffordshire.

They were originally a bird to be found principally in mountain districts, but this no longer applies; solitary large trees and old quarry workings will suffice. They are a shy and vigilant bird, pair for life and feed on carrion, eggs, young birds, rabbits, and rodents. They are resident in the UK.

RAZORBILL. L 37 – 39 cm. WS 63 – 67 cm.
A bold black and white bird, with a distinctive large black and white lined bill, which quickly distinguishes it from the guillemot.

They are a cliff nesting species frequently nesting next to guillemots, where the differences in bill shape help in identification; they are not as common as the guillemot however. They are a relatively silent bird although a deep creaking 'urrr' is heard from breeding birds.

Another marine bird only regularly seen on land during the breeding season, when they are to be found on steep sea cliffs. They return to breed early in February – March and leave their breeding sites by late July. Rarely seen inland, spending their life at sea, where they feed on fish. All the auks are good swimmers and all their food is obtained from the sea.

RED-LEGGED PARTRIDGE. L 32 – 34 cm. WS 45 – 50 cm.
Another introduced species. They originate from the continent, and were once known as the French partridge. Red-legged partridge proved to breed very successfully in captivity, unlike our native partridge, the grey partridge, and are bred for shooting purposes, much like the pheasant. As all the released birds do not get shot, they have established themselves as a wild bird, and are now more common than the grey partridge.

They are a bird of open country, farmland, heaths and lower mountain slopes, where their call is regularly heard, a 'kcho, kcho,kcho, kcho' followed by a 'kochoko-koke, kochoko-koke'. Easily identified, when seen, by their contrastingly marked head, grey-brown back and red legs, hence the name. Quite a colourful looking bird.

They are residents and feed on seeds, plant matter and insects, and a family group, (a covey) will remain together until the next breeding season.

REDSHANK. L 27 – 29 cm. WS 45 – 52 cm.

After the lapwing, probably the commonest wader seen inland. A grey-brown bird with bright orange-red legs and red base to long bill. The plumage is covered with dark spots, markings which apparently are more pronounced in northern populations. In winter the plumage is more uniformly grey brown above with underparts paler. In flight they show a white trailing edge to wings.

When breeding they are very active and noisy birds, and if alarmed they utter a persistent 'klu, klu, klu' alarm call, which alerts other birds nearby to danger.

They are a resident in the UK although we get passage birds moving through March – April and migrants from further north return October – November, many of which are birds of passage.

In the UK nests on wet meadows, coastal grasslands, boggy heaths and moors. On passage and during winter a common bird on shallow shores and inland wetlands.

REDWING. L 21 cm.

A common winter migrant to the UK from Scandinavia, frequently associating with the fieldfare, and are regularly seen in large flocks on fields and in open woods.

A feature about this bird is the fact it normally migrates at night, so it is safe to presume it navigates by the stars.

In appearance it is quite similar to the song thrush, but the distinctive facial markings with pronounced pale supercilium, (eyebrow) and whitish stripes beneath the cheeks, quickly separating the two. The bird also has rusty-red flanks, seen when the bird is perched, and in flight the rusty-red underwing really does stand out if compared with the song thrush.

When on migration, which is during September and October, flocks can be heard as they pass over, when a protracted, indrawn 'tsueep' rings out. Birds which migrate in the dark keep in constant contact by calls and these calls can be heard in cities as they pass through.

It is a scarce breeding bird, mainly in Scotland, but a common and widespread winter visitor, regularly seen in gardens and parks where berries are available. Cotoneaster is a definite favourite for this bird, and a small flock will quickly strip a bush bare. They depart April, early May.

REED BUNTING. L 15.5 cm.

Our commonest bunting which breeds in wetlands among osiers and reeds and dryer sites especially among young conifers, where its thin indrawn 'tseeu' call is a good indicaion of its presence. Frequently perches on the top of reeds and other plants, and if disturbed often jerks its tail as it dives down seeking cover.

The male bird is unmistakable amongst our native birds, having a black head and throat, white collar and drooping moustache, with a black stubby bill. The female is a brownish looking bird, with buffy-white and dark streaking to her plumage. In winter they moult and the male loses the black head although the white collar and moustache are still visible, making confusion between the sexes likely.

In recent years has become a regular garden visitor, mainly during winter. It is a resident in the UK, although numbers increase during the winter when visitors arrive from the continent, and they remain from September until May.

REED WARBLER. L 12.5 cm.

The commonest warbler found near to water, during the breeding season rarely seen away from reed beds and the like. A bird frequently heard, but not seen much regularly. Just a movement in a reed bed is all that may betray its presence apart from the grating and nasal notes. Not musical in any way, but unlikely to be missed, as it vibrates out. It is a very active bird, constantly moving through the reeds which is a great help in seeing the bird. The call can be confused with that of the sedge warbler, but if the call is coming from reeds growing in water, it is safe to presume it is the reed; sedge warbler are rarely seen over water, contrary to their name.

The reed warbler has a rather pointed head with a flat forehead and a rather long pointed bill for the size of the bird. Overall brown above with underparts a buff - white, and the head has a short pale supercilium, difficult to see at times.

A summer migrant, arriving from mid-April, departing August through to October.

ROBIN. L 14 cm.

No description is required for this bird. Everyone knows the robin as the plump, upright bird, sporting a red breast, which hops about on your back lawn.

Shyness is no part of the make up for this bird. Sexes are similar. The juveniles are very spotted and lack the red breast, but posture quickly identifies them for what they are.

Although a woodland species they are common in gardens, where they both feed and breed, very tolerant to man which probably explains their success. When in Europe birding, I have found the robin to be a more shy bird, nowhere as near accommodating as our bird.

They have the longest period of song of all our native birds, which is the reason they are our most territorial of birds, and even in winter they will chase fellow robins away. They also have two distinctive types of song. In the summer it is a rippling stream of clear, sweet notes, with changes in tempo; winter is much quieter and sounds almost melancholy. When hidden away in shrubbery you can frequently hear a 'tic, tic, tic' being uttered.

They are resident in the UK, although we do get visitors from the continent in the winter.

ROOK. L 47 cm.

The commonest of the crow family, and is very distinctive due to the odd gait and bushy trousers covering the top of the leg. Has a peaked crown and a long, pale coloured bill, quite pointed, almost dagger-like, with a grey base to bill. On the carrion crow the bill is black and it lacks the bushy trousers.

They are colonial breeding birds and in many cases their rookery can be many years old. In my village, where I have lived for nearly sixty years, the rookery is still in the same area as it was when I first arrived, although a second small rookery was started six years ago. This now has twelve nests.

They are regularly seen on open farm fields, and open grasslands where they forage for worms, insects and vegetable matter. They also take young birds and eggs where possible, but eat less carrion than the carrion crow. Rarely seen singularly, but do be careful as carrion crows will flock up in the winter.

They are a resident bird in the UK, although many continental birds visit us during the winter, from September to April.

SANDERLING. L 20 – 21 cm. WS 36 – 39 cm.

A bird from the high Arctic, and a bird of both passage and a winter visitor.

Regularly seen in large flocks on sandy beaches, mud flats and water near the coast.

Unusual inland. When seen on beaches it has the delightful habit of almost dancing with the tide as it flows in and out. Dancing it is not, needless to say, searching for food it is.

During the winter when we see the bird, it is probably the palest wader you will see in any number. Look for the black, rather stout looking bill and black legs which contrast with the white head and white underparts. Upper parts very pale grey.

In the summer, and occasionally, a few do delay their departure north. They are a much darker looking bird with the upper parts being a rusty-red, this to a varying degree, with the head and upper breast also having this rusty-red tinge. In flight and in all plumage conditions, has a broad black bordered white wing-bar.

I have found them to be a very confiding bird and have studied them from very close distances, definitely a bird to enjoy. Where they breed they probably do not come into contact with man that frequently.

SAND MARTIN. L 12 cm.

Very much a brown and white bird, although at distance and depending upon light conditions, may look almost black, very similar to the house martin, but lacks the white rump of that species. Frequently associates with the house martin and swallow when feeding over open water, and here usually it is the bird feeding in the lowest flight, just skimming the water level.

They are a colonial breeding species and are to be found in vertical sand or earth banks in gravel pits and river banks. Here they will dig out a long horizontal tunnel, sometimes a metre deep, for their nest. Some of the larger colonies have many hundred pairs in attendance.

Although a summer migrant, there are repeated reports of occasional birds being seen in southern England throughout the winter. They are one of our earliest summer arrivals arriving as early as March, and leaving any time from August. When on their return migration, large concentrations of sand martins may be seen, particularly in dense reed beds, where they roost. Some new field guides now refer to this bird as the common sand martin.

SEDGE WARBLER. L 13 cm.

Easily identifiable with its conspicuous greyish-white supercilium with the dark stripe through the eye and dark crown. If only heard can be confused with reed warbler, but once recognised, you realise the sedge is more lively and varied wth long trills, not as repetitive as the reed's calls.

Although associated with water it is usually found nesting in rank shore vegetation with bushes and overgrown ditches. It is also more frequently seen singing in the open on top of a bush, shrub or other taller vegetation, definitely more accommodating than the reed warbler. It is also more solitary than the reed which frequently breeds in loose colonies.

It is a summer migrant returning to the UK to breed and arrives April to May, departing August to early October. It is widespread apart from mountainous areas and the food is mainly insects.

Definitely a bird to listen out for when near to overgrown areas close to water, especially still water.

SHELDUCK. L 58 – 71 cm. WS 110 – 135 cm.

A large and boldly marked duck of just three main colours. Blackish head and upper neck, tinged green, noticeable especially in good sunlight, red bill; the drake has a pronounced red knob at base of bill; the female lacks this; a broad rust-brown band across the breast, similar colour lower belly and black on back and wings, with remainder of plumage white. No mistaking this bird.

Due to their size they were once thought to be geese, and were known as sheld geese. They are a widespread species which in recent years have commenced to breed well inland; any large lake or reservoir is likely to have a pair or two breeding.

They breed in holes, rabbit burrows, holes under walls and buildings, and where near farmland have nested in hay stacks and occasional reports of using dog kennels.

What the dog thought about that is another matter.

A very interesting feature about adult shelducks is the fact that birds will congregate in June – July to have a mass moult. Thousands of birds visit the Waddenzee area to moult and smaller numbers do so in Bridgewater Bay. They leave their ducklings in the care of 'foster parents', where large crèches of young birds are cared for.

A resident in the UK, although much movement takes place due to moult behaviour. Note, frequently now referred to as the common shelduck.

SHOVELER. L 49 – 52 cm. WS 70 – 84 cm.

Instantly recognised by the large bill with a very broad tip, hence the name, some new books now call this the northern shoveler.

At distance the drake's head looks black, although when viewed closely this is green, white breast, belly and flanks a bold chestnut, with the upper forewing a pale blue. The duck is similarly marked to the mallard duck and the upper forewing is a pale dullish grey.

Although seen here in most months of the year, the majority of UK breeding birds migrate to the Mediterranean in July to October, returning March to April, being replaced by winter migrants from north and eastern Europe. They are rarely seen in flocks, usually seen in pairs or very small parties.

Found on lowland lakes, reservoirs, marshy meadows and flooded grasslands, not seen too often along the coast, very much a freshwater duck in Britain. They feed on plankton, crustaceans, insects and seeds which they filter through their large bills.

They are a surface feeding bird who stir up the water with their feet enabling them to feed. Specialised feeders in fact.

SISKIN. L 12 cm.

A distinctively marked bird, especially the male. He is contrastingly marked black, yellow and green, colours which really do stand out. The female is duller but she too has the yellow on the wings which distinguish her. Both have very sharp pointed bills which enable them to extract seeds easily from between pine cone scales.

Predominantly found in conifer plantation during the breeding season. In winter will join in with flocks of mixed titmice when they are to be seen feeding on alder seed heads.

In the UK they are seen more frequently during the breeding season in northern areas, and their numbers increase each winter with visitors from eastern and northern Europe; these usually arrive September and depart by May.

Over recent years they have become very much a garden visitor during the winter months when they regularly visit garden feeders; a very infrequent garden breeder due to their preference for conifer plantations.

SKYLARK. L 18 – 19 cm.

One of our true vocal species, whose song is unmistakable. A continuous stream of trilling and babbling notes, mostly given from on high as the bird hovers, on quivering wings, the true sound of the countryside. Difficult to describe phonetically, but Vaughan Williams got close with his beautiful work 'The Lark Ascending'. One of the few birds which will sing all day, from first light to dusk.

A bird which has unfortunately decreased in numbers over recent years, as farming techniques and land usage have reduced their breeding territories, no longer a common bird.

They are a ground nesting species and if you are fortunate enough to stumble across a nesting bird they frequently run away from the nest and will feign having a broken wing to draw you away from the nest. When returning to the nest they rarely fly directly to it, landing some distance away and running to the nest under cover of vegetation.

Feeds on insects, invertebrates, plant matter and seeds. In the UK it is a resident and we also have birds of passage and winter visitors. They will flock up during autumn and winter along with these winter visitors and these flocks are to be seen on stubble and ploughed fields, mainly in England and Wales.

SNIPE. L 25 – 27 cm WS 37 – 43 cm.

Now referred to as the common snipe, I only wish it was so. Their numbers have, sadly, plummeted recently as much of their breeding territories have been taken over. In my youth they were almost a resident on any marsh, bog or wet meadows with short vegetation, not any more unfortunately.

They are a plump looking wader with a long bill and very pronounced head markings. It probes deep in the mud and soft ground with very jerky movements. If threatened it normally squats using its plumage as camouflage until it explodes into the air uttering harsh 'ketsch' calls as it does so.

The breeding display is quite something. They are aerial displays of combined fluttering climbs and dives, accompanied by a humming sound produced by the vibration of the outer tail feathers. Unmistakable when witnessed, makes identification easy. Their song is a loud but rhythmic 'tick-a, tick-a, tick-a' regularly given from the top of a fence post or tree.

They are more active at dawn and dusk, and although resident in the UK we do have passage birds and winter visitors from northern Europe. During winter look for them in muddy areas.

SONG THRUSH. L 23 cm.
One of our most popular song birds, once very common, not so now unfortunately. Well spread in gardens, parks and woodland, mainly broad leaved.

A regular feature on lawned areas especially after rain has fallen and worms are brought nearer to the surface.

It is a rather compact looking bird, relatively short-tailed, well spotted throat, breast and underparts, brown above. In flight has a rather jerky motion, which helps in identification compared with redwing or mistle thrush.

Feeds on worms, snails, insects, fruits and berries. You frequently come across a song thrush's 'anvil'. A stone or piece of rock where the song thrush has smashed snails open so they could be eaten.

A resident in the UK, plus birds of passage and winter visitors from northern and central Europe. Occasionally seen mixed in with flocks of redwings and fieldfares during the winter, it is presumed these may well have been accompanying migrants.

They build a very interesting nest, often well concealed in ivy and the like, an intricate moss-clad bowl lined with mud. A substantial nest for any bird.

Most aptly named, along with the blackbird, one of our most popular song birds, without it, a dawn chorus would not be complete.

SPARROWHAWK. L 28 – 38 cm. WS 60 – 75 cm.
A relatively small raptor, frequently confused with kestrel, but sparrowhawks do not hover, they pursue their prey, and can do so with speed. Normal flight pattern is a series of rapid wing beats, alternating with glides when the wings look half closed.

They are a widespread species in both town and country, and where birds are regularly fed they can become a bit of a nuisance as they prey on the smaller garden species. This however is how nature intended, and it is a measure of the intelligence of the hawk to be able to use this. It certainly provides the onlooker with a marvellous opportunity to watch a bird of prey go about its business.

Sparrowhawks are a tree nesting species, unlike the kestrel which will also nest in or on buildings, and will newly build their nest each year, not just add to it as do other birds of prey. They appear to have a preference for conifers. Their diet is birds, caught both on the ground and in flight, along with the occasional mammal.

Will rarely, if ever, eat carrion.

When perched have a rather upright stance when the barring on the breast is very conspicuous, especially on the female who is a generally grey looking bird. The male, although also being grey, has rufous cheeks and breast.

They are a resident, and adult birds are fairly sedentary, remaining in their territory throughout the year. We have occasional birds of passage and winter visitors.

The young birds will move quite a distance seeking out territories of their own.

STARLING. L 21 cm.

The avian equivalent of man. Every attribute found in us is repeated with the starling, the good, the bad and the ugly! It even walks, whereas many birds hop. But what a bird. If any bird has learned to live alongside man, this is it, and long may it continue to do so.

Without starlings no garden would be complete, in my opinion.

Considering it started out as a woodland species it is now most definitely seen more on farmland or in suburban areas. They can form enormous flocks after breeding, well into their thousands and these can be seen wheeling round in the sky, especially at dusk and at their roosting sites. Many of these birds are winter visitors from north and north eastern Europe. These flocks are known as 'murmurations'.

If you have a lawn at home, you will be familiar with its habit of probing lawns with its long conical bill, to find worms and insects, and how it regularly inspects the hole it has made. When large numbers of starlings visit your lawn the well-perforated ground bears witness to their activity. As well as worms and insects it also feeds on berries, seeds and fruit, and regularly visits bird feeders, they also forage on any scraps man puts out. Nothing is wasted with this bird.

The starling is unlikely to be confused with any other bird we see in the UK, and an adult male is a most colourful bird, black basically but covered with multi - coloured spots.

They nest in holes in trees, walls, buildings and suitable nest boxes, and their calls are most varied and they are very good mimics with sounds of curlew, lapwing, magpie and house sparrow in their vocabulary. Some bird.

Many new field guides now call this the common starling.

Should you holiday in south west Europe you may come across the starling's cousin, the spotless starling; this bird in summer plumage has no spots.

STOCK DOVE. L 32 – 34 cm. WS 63 – 69 cm.

Probably the most over-looked bird we have. Easily confused with feral pigeons which at times it closely compares. Similar in colour to the woodpigeon, but lacks the white neck and has a shorter tail. Flight is steady but fast, not the clatter associated with the woodpigeon. In flight, lacks the black wing bar of the feral pigeon and the white of the woodpigeon.

It breeds in wooded areas and forest edges, parks with mature oaks and open areas with isolated mature trees which provide holes for nesting. Locally can be seen on rocky coasts and occasionally on buildings.

Occurs sparsely, but where seen is usually common, and will flock up readily after breeding, in far looser flocks than that of the woodpigeon, and then favours agricultural land for feeding, here associating with woodpigeons.

Food: berries, seeds, buds, beechmast and in gardens will come to feeders where it feeds on fallen grain and the like. Here, if you see the bird take off you will hear the wings clapping as it takes to the air, and the whistling sound of the wings once in flight.

A resident in the UK, although there is a movement from northern Europe in the winter.

SWALLOW. L 19 – 22 cm.

The herald of summer, our most eagerly anticipated of the summer migrants, with its long forked tail, recognised by all. If two birds typify summer for most people, it has to be the swallow and cuckoo.

Upper parts a blue glossy black with white underparts, blue-black breast-band with red throat and forehead gives the bird a distinctive appearance, especially when combined with the deeply forked tail and long, thin elongated tail streamers.

New field guides now list them as the barn swallow, which is understandable, so many do nest in barns and similar out buildings. Here they build their half-cup shaped nest of mud on rafters, beams and the like. They are very faithful to these sites and will return to them annually, and it is not uncommon to have several pairs nesting in the same building, and they are very tolerant of people working in these buildings.

They arrive from the end of March and usually depart from August to October, depending upon how many broods they have reared. There are more frequent reports of their being seen in southern England in mid-winter, so a few may be attempting to overwinter in the UK. Being insect eaters, I would not consider their success rate to be high, but it is probably an indication of 'climate change'.

One may not make a summer, but it is a good indication that summer is not far away.

SWIFT. L 16 – 17 cm. WS 42 – 48 cm.

By many, thought to be a relative of the swallow and martins, but comes from an entirely different family, and is probably the most unique bird we have the pleasure of experiencing. It is totally adapted to life in the air and the only time it is not flying is when it is nesting and incubating eggs.

Feeds on flying insects and spiders which it catches in its large gape. It will range far and near as it seeks food, frequently flying long distances when food is short. In these conditions they can fall into an energy-saving torpor, and can survive for up to 10 – 15 days without food; if this occurs as a young bird they cease to grow.

Around their breeding sites, the roofs of houses and the like, they are regularly seen performing flights at 'dizzy' speeds, frequently in formation, rolling and screaming as they go. Due to this piercing call, birders frequently refer to them as 'screechers'.

They are here for a relatively short period. Arriving late April into

May, and leaving from July to early September, so enjoy them whilst you can.

TAWNY OWL. L 37 – 39 cm. WS 94 – 104 cm.
The original hooting owl, who does not feel excited to hear the 'PooOOH' followed shortly by 'poo, poo-ho-ho. HOOO'O'O'O'O'O', the latter part of the phrase really drawn out. A true call of the night, and certainly one to raise the hairs on the back of your neck.

A plump owl with large black eyes which stare straight ahead from a head that appears to have no neck. A general red-brown in colour. When seen in flight the wings look quite short, and when gliding, as they do a lot, these are held slightly down curved.

Breeds in open mixed woodlands, large gardens, parks, and avenues of trees, as long as the trees have ready made holes for nesting. They are the commonest owl found near to human habitations.

As they are strictly nocturnal, it is usually dusk before they are out hunting, although they can be seen during the day at their daytime roost, usually pressed hard against a tree trunk. If located by other birds their alarm calls are a good indication of one being found. Titmice and blackbirds are particularly agitated by a roosting owl.

They are a resident, and quite sedentary once they reach adulthood. Feeds mainly on rodents, but will also take birds, frogs, worms and larger insects.

TREECREEPER. L 12.5 cm.
Very much a woodland species where it feeds solely on the trees. A very nimble and delicate looking bird which climbs spirally up the trunks of trees, frequently pausing to search out for suitable insects. It then flits down low in another tree to repeat the process. Unlike the nuthatch, never works down the trunk, only climbs up.

It builds the nest beneath loose bark; from this you can appreciate the bird is more likely to be seen amongst more mature trees, principally deciduous, than saplings and the like.

The bird is a general brownish on upper parts with a white throat, chest and underparts. It has a thin bill suitable for easing out insects from the bark and long claws which enable it to cling to the bark of the trees. It is a very agile and active feeder.

In the winter often accompanies flocks of titmice, and occasionally will visit feeders, but being principally an insect eater, rarely takes seed and the like.

In the UK they are predominantly a resident, although on the continent, especially eastern regions, there is some migration.

TREE PIPIT. L 15 cm.

Very similar to the meadow pipit and best told by voice and behaviour. As can be told by the name, the bird associates with trees, not necessarily woodlands, but areas where trees are to be found. It has favourite trees which it will use as perches for singing and launch pads for aerial vocal performances.

When seen clearly has a longer bill than the meadow, a more distinctive yellow sub-moustachial stripe and courser breast streaking, but as mentioned earlier, song and behaviour is the better guide, as their territories can overlap, especially where trees are growing on open moorland.

They are a summer migrant and bird of passage, and can be seen on meadows and freshwater margins when on passage, frequently along with meadow pipits.

TREE SPARROW. L 14 cm.

Not seen so frequently as was once, but hopefully with the concentration on tree planting now taking place, given time the situation should improve.

Distinguished from the house sparrow by the wholly red-brown crown (in the house sparrow this is black) the black face patch and a white band across the nape.

Sexes are similar.

Not a town bird, occurs more in open farmland where it occasionally nests in nest boxes, but mainly in tree holes, normally on woodland edges or in small clumps of trees, being the principal nesting sites. Not a bird of thick woodland.

They are more mobile than house sparrows and will join in with finches and buntings on fields and arable land during the winter. When in flight their fast 'tek, tek, tek,' identifies them.

They are big seed eaters and will come to garden bird feeders to obtain these, especially in the winter months. Insects are also taken.

Resident in the UK, with small numbers of birds migrating to us during winter, mainly from northern Europe.

TUFTED DUCK. L 40 – 47 cm. WS 67 – 73 cm.
Our commonest breeding diving duck on freshwater locations. The drake is black with a brilliant white belly and long drooping black crest, the female being a more uniform dark brown. The drake can be confused with a drake scaup, but the scaup has a grey back compared with the black back of the tufted and also lacks the crest.

Regularly seen on lakes and ponds with shore vegetation, where they dive for molluscs and plant matter. During the winter months large flocks can collect at certain locations on open waters, reservoirs, the larger lakes and in sheltered sea bays.

Our resident population is bolstered by migrants, especially during the winter months, and are to be seen all year round on many a park pool, where at times they can outnumber the resident mallard population.

WAXWING. L 18 cm.
If ever a bird is unmistakable, this is it, one of the most exotic birds to be seen in the UK. To try to describe the bird is most difficult, just Google it and you will see why I say that.

It is a bird which arrives in the UK in fluctuating numbers, few some years, many others, this is dependent on the food supply in their native countries, Scandinavia and north eastern Europe. Here their diet is insects in the summer, which it captures in flight, and in the winter feeds on berries, especially rowan berries and Swedish whitebeam. If this crop fails then migration takes place to warmer climates, hence they arrive here.

With our berry crop being very wide, cultivated and wild, they can be widespread. Garden berry trees, such as cotoneaster, really do attract this bird, and where there is enough of it, large numbers will call in to feed.

Their flight is very similar to that of a starling, so it always pays to look closely at what you think may be starlings, especially during the winter months, as you could be in for a great surprise.

They arrive from the end of October returning April onwards.

WILLOW WARBLER. L 11.5 cm.
After the swallows and martins, these, along with the chiffchaff, are

probably the next most common summer migrants, although only experienced bird watchers regularly see or hear them.

Similar to the chiffchaff in appearance, although it is a yellower looking bird, especially on throat, breast, and supercilium and has distinctive paler legs. The most positive means of identification is by voice. The willow warbler has a delightful and sweet song phrase which descends and falls away in clear notes. I frequently compare it to water gently falling down a shallow waterfall. An important part of any woodland dawn chorus.

A common bird in all types of woodland and scrub with scattered deciduous trees, rarely heard or seen in conifer plantations. As with all the warblers, they are big insect eaters.

As well as breeding in the UK we have birds of passage pass through and they arrive during April and leave by the end of October.

Certainly one to listen out for, which in many cases is far easier than looking hard for the bird once the trees are in leaf.

WILLOW TIT. L 11.5 cm.
The last of our five common titmice, and the least common. Very similar in appearance to the marsh tit, the principal differences being a larger looking head with a dull black crown and larger black bib and a pale white wing bar on the upper wing surfaces.

Voice again is important to help separate the two species. The willow tit has a characteristic, drawn out and harsh sounding CHAY – CHAY – CHAY – CHAY' or 'tsi- ti- CHAY – CHAY'.

I have long considered that the names of the willow and marsh should be changed. The willow tit prefers to inhabit swampy deciduous woodland along streams and lake shores.

They are resident in the UK, and feed on insects, seeds and berries. Not so frequently recorded as a garden bird as is the marsh tit.

WOODPIGEON. L 40 – 42 cm. WS 75 – 80 cm.
The largest and commonest of our native doves, instantly recognisable by the white markings on the neck and wings. A uniformally grey looking bird with black wingtips and black tail.

The numbers have increased dramatically in recent years, and many people consider it to be a pest, especially the farming community.

Widespread and found in all kinds of woodland, parks, gardens and towns, one of the commonest birds seen in built up areas.

On taking to flight the wings make a loud clatter, and in display flight it climbs on clattering wings to glide down on stiff wings, quite distinctive. The typical call is a 'doo-doooh, doo doo-du', and carries quite a distance. Five notes compared with the collared dove's three.

Feeds on berries, seeds, buds, beech mast and acorns, and are regular garden feeders, where seed and scraps are eagerly sought. In my garden they have a preference for sunflower hearts. Forages regularly in the morning and evenings on fields.

In the winter they form large flocks and these may be joined by migrants from the continent.

WREN. L 9.5 cm.
After the firecrest and goldcrest, our smallest bird.

Unmistakable, a small rusty-brown bird with a cocked up tail, as familiar as a robin.

As well as being one of our smallest birds, it is also one of the commonest, if not the most common.

It is abundant in woodlands with thick ground vegetation, gardens, parks, open scrubby areas, on farmland and also in reedbeds. Very much a bird of the ground where it can hide away in dense shrubbery and will be seen rushing about on the ground most actively.

The loud and penetrating call is what regularly draws attention to the bird, this being a prolonged, excited and loud sound which makes you wonder how a bird so small could have such a powerful voice.

In many new field guides it is now referred to as the winter wren, the reason for which I just cannot understand as it is resident and seen all year.

YELLOWHAMMER. L 16.5 cm.
Known to many by its characteristic call 'a bit of bread and no cheeeeeese'.

Many books refer to this as a melancholy sounding 'tzi-tzi-tzi-tzi-tzi-tzi-tzuuh' I cannot agree with the word melancholy, to me it is the typical sound of farmland. As a young lad in my egg collecting days, we used to refer to this bird as 'the scribbly schoolmaster' due to the scribble like markings on the birds eggs.

Not as common and widespread as it used to be, but seen in open country with hedges, large gardens, especially if overgrown, juniper slopes in the far north and thorny scrubland. In the winter will form up small flocks and these regularly visit farmyards and stubble. One to look out for as well as hearing.

It is a largish bunting, long-tailed with yellow on the head and a rusty-red rump. The female is paler, almost lacking the yellow.

They are resident in the UK, but do flock up with other finches and buntings in the winter months, when they may include the odd winter visitor from northern Europe. Birds breeding in the northern UK will also move southwards each winter, although they do not leave the country.

YELLOW WAGTAIL. L 18 – 19 cm.
A long-tailed canary if there ever was. Very aptly named, predominantly a yellow and green looking bird. There are several races of the yellow wagtail so they always have to be studied closely. Fortunately, the majority of the European races have dark head colours, and when seen, these do stand out. For those who like scientific names, ours is *Motacilla flava flavissima*.

Breeds on damp meadows and marsh fringes, ground nesting. In autumn will flock up and can be seen on pastureland, especially where cattle are feeding, and follow the cattle around as they disturb insects whilst they feed.

They are a summer migrant arriving March – June, and depart August – October, and it is during these times of the year that you may pick up one of the continental races, so look out for yellow wagtails with dark looking heads. But do not confuse them with the grey wagtail, that is the only one with a grey back.

There, we have looked at a hundred or so of our more regularly seen species, with the odd more unusual bird included amongst them. When visiting parks you are likely to meet up with escapees and birds which are now living in a semi-wild condition, and in time could become fully wild birds like the Canada goose has become. They rarely migrate as far as the UK. All of the birds we now see are due to escapees or releases made over the years. There are other following suit, so let us now look at some of these.

CHAPTER II.

RELEASES AND ESCAPEES.

The majority of these are likely to be waterfowl. If these birds are not pinioned as young birds, once they learn to fly they will be off, and if enough do and they meet up, breeding will occur, and given time they become accepted as British birds. In recent times three in particular have done so, two ducks, the mandarin and the ruddy duck, along with the ring-necked parakeet; yes, we have parrots now living in the wild in the UK.

So let us now have a look at some of these:-

BAR-HEADED GOOSE. L 70 – 83 cm. WS 150 – 160 cm.
A bird native to central Asia and is famous for the fact it migrates southwards every year over the Himalayas, the highest height recorded by any bird. They breed in enormous flocks of thousands of birds, but have been introduced in one or two of the European countries, Norway and Holland for instance, where they are now breeding successfully in the wild. For a bird used to migrating large distances, some of the birds we see could well be wild birds from across the North Sea.

They are an attractive looking goose, very pale grey and their distinctive white heads have two black bars crossing the back of the head, one running back from the eyes, the other lower on the head. Bar-heads are small billed, yellow in colour, as are their legs. When seen in flight they are largely whitish looking.

A smart looking bird in many respects, neat and tidy.

BARNACLE GOOSE. L 58 – 70 cm. WS 132 – 145 cm.
The smallest of geese seen regularly. Large numbers visit the UK each winter, mainly seen in Scotland, but thanks to escapees and the like, now a bird seen frequently in scattered flocks throughout the year. These feral birds do not migrate so consequently you can come across them on many

a large stretch of water, normally in small flocks. After many years of breeding in captivity these birds lose their instincts of migration, and become residents, as has happened to the Canada goose.

They are basically a three coloured bird, black, white and grey. They are a compact looking goose, for their size quite thick-set with a short black neck and white faced. Underparts a silvery - white with upper-parts grey with black and white barring.

When seen in flight they frequently call to each other, and this is a barking 'ka'or 'kaw'.

Flocks are very mobile and will move from water to water. As locally to where I live in Staffordshire, we have a flock seen regularly at the J.C.B Lakes at Rocester, and these birds commute across the county border into Derbyshire, where they can be seen at Carsington Water.

Their true homes are Arctic islands and coasts, preferably rocky and steep sloped, and arrive here October to early November, and return north April to May.

These geese are obviously on the British List due to their winter migration here, but birds seen during summer are feral.

BLACK SWAN. L 110 – 142 CM. WS 160 – 200cm.
Native of Australia, has long been a common bird in collections and has been introduced in other countries of the world. In Australia it is frequently seen in very large flocks, numbering over a thousand at times, and is very mobile depending upon food etc.

An instantly recognised bird, being black with white primaries and a yellow bill. It is also a rather aggressive bird and will attack smaller species. Features in most collections.

It is regularly seen on many a park pool and some of these birds are free flying, having not been pinioned when cygnets. Reports of their breeding in the wild are recorded, but as yet it has not been accepted as a British bird; to do so it needs to become completely self-sufficient, but I think it will only be a matter of time before it becomes a British bird.

Should you holiday near to Dawlish, look out for this bird as Dawlish has for a long time had many of these birds roaming free.

MUSCOVY. L 66 – 84 cm. WS 158 – 163 cm
Native to the tropical forest lakes and rivers in Central and South

America, but familiar in its domestic form, where it has been kept for many years and is now a regular sight on most farmyards, as well as a resident on park pools.

The drake is larger than the duck with a pronounced knob at the base of the bill. Plumage may be varied on domestic birds, but they are easily identified as muscovies by their naked, warty faces with a reddish bill and legs. Although the plumage is similar in both sexes, the drake has a short mane on the head. In a true wild state they are a much sleeker bird.

They are a relatively silent species, although the drake will hiss if annoyed and the duck has a short, weak quack.

Not often seen in flight, they normally prefer to swim away, but when seen in flight they are a chunky looking bird with broad white coverts on both wing surfaces.

In many respects not an attractive looking bird, but very distinctive. Enough are now breeding in the wild for it to be included as a British bird in the not too distant future.

RED-CRESTED POCHARD. L 53 – 57 cm. WS 84 – 88 cm.
An attractive and popular bird among collections, and an occasional migrant from the continent, so it is on the British List. Breeds in scattered location across Europe, usually on lowland lakes with dense vegetation.

There has been a slow spread of its breeding range in recent years and reports consider Spain to be the most popular area. In the UK escapees have commenced to breed in several areas, the Cotswolds being a particular area. In the area generally known as the Cotswold Water Park, large flocks of 40 or 50 birds are regularly seen, and all thanks to escapees breeding over the years. Where they are found they tend to be residential.

They are a smart looking bird, the drake has a very striking pale red bill and red head which contrasts with the black neck, breast and stern with a distinctive white patch. The back is brown and when in flight a bright white wing bar is visible on rear of upper wing surface. The female, although not as brightly coloured, also shows this wing bar.

RING-NECKED PARAKEET. L 38 – 42 cm. WS 42 – 48 cm.
The only species of parrot to be seen in the UK, and this is all down to escapees and deliberate releases. There are various stories of how this bird came to appear in the UK, the most likely is release of the bird. In

captivity they are very noisy birds and many owners grew tired of them and let them fly free, but the best reason I have heard is put down to the filming of 'The African Queen'

The story I heard was that Shepperton Studios, who made the film, brought in a lot of ring-necked parakeets to create background jungle noises and that over the period of several day's filming, many of the birds escaped. Finding conditions perfect, they survived and bred successfully. From latest reports I understand that we now have in excess of 20,000 birds in the UK, and from their start in London and the Home Counties, they can now be seen in northern England.

They are an all-green bird, long-tailed with a black and pink neck-band, hence the name. Where they breed in number there is concern that they are affecting local bird populations, as they have an aggressive behaviour and will drive other birds away from food.

An attractive and unusual bird, but not one to be loved unfortunately.

You will find this bird referred to in some new field guides as the rose-ringed parakeet, and it is obviously now on the British List.

RUDDY DUCK. L 35 – 43 cm. WS 53 – 62 cm.
A native of North America, which due to release and escapees from collections, spread rapidly over England. The West Midlands became the stronghold for this delightful little duck. Unfortunately it is a close relative to the very rare white-headed duck, and it was reported that the ruddy had mated with white-headed ducks in Spain, and if this was allowed to continue would affect the numbers of a very rare species. Consequently, an eradication programme was instigated and the elimination of the ruddy commenced.

This, needless to say, caused an uproar in the bird watching world here in the UK. The reason why the white-headed duck was so rare was due to two things, none of which had anything to do with the ruddy duck, they had been shot almost out of existence and habitats had been destroyed.

Now the ruddy duck is a rare bird, so few escaped the gun, and I know if any birders see one, they tell no one else.

They are a dapper little diving duck who hold their tails stiffly erect, we call them stifftails. The drake ruddy is a compact looking bird with a large head and blue bill, the body is a deep chestnut, it has a black crown and hind neck combined with a white face. The female is plainer and lacks the head and face markings of the drake, she being brown and off-white with a dark stripe across the cheeks.

Obviously on the British List, although now almost extinct.

RUDDY SHELDUCK. L 61 – 67 cm. WS 121 – 145 cm.

A rare visitor to the UK from east Europe and western Asia, so when seen it is almost safe to presume the bird to be an escapee. It is a regular captive bird in collections and escapes do occur.

They are a large duck with a distinctive and uniformly rust coloured plumage on the body, a pale head, creamy-white, a pronounced black bill, rump, tail and flight feathers black, and the drake has a black neck ring during the breeding season. The duck is similarly plumed but has a whiter face and lacks the neck ring. In flight they display a pure white forewing on both wing surfaces, a very distinctive feature.

In the wild they are to be found in a variety of inland habitats, on vast steppes at the shores of lakes, on saltmarshes, along rivers and on hills. They have also been reported breeding on rocky mountains far from water. They nest in holes, natural or in buildings, and are very migratory and fly at considerable height.

A bird I always consider to be smart and tidy looking, and obviously on the British List as we occasionally get rare visitors.

SNOW GOOSE. L 65 – 78 cm. WS 130 – 160 cm.

A North American species which breeds in the Arctic tundra, as the name implies, and migrates as far south as Mexico. True wild birds are very rare in the UK, but as the bird is a regular captive bred bird, they do escape. In Scotland there is a feral flock breeding and records have occurred of their breeding at other locations in the UK.

They are a pure white bird with black wing tips, although there is a phase, called the 'blue goose' in America, which is dark grey with a white head and silver - grey wing-coverts.

They are very vocal, especially on migration when they can be in flocks of several thousands, and these birds can be heard well over a mile away. To see geese in these numbers would indeed be a spectacle.

There are several races of snow geese, and in the UK you are likely to see a smaller looking bird, similarly marked; this is the Ross's goose. This bird is more the size of a shelduck.

Another bird on the British List due to the odd rare vagrant.

WHITE-FACED WHISTLING DUCK. L 43 – 48 cm. WS. 86 – 94 cm.
A native to the African and South American continents where it can be seen in very large flocks during the day on stretches of open water.

The generally dark plumage contrasting with the white head clearly identify this bird, not that you will find it in any British field guide. It rarely perches and is a good swimmer, walker and diver, and feeds by dabbling in shallow waters. Although flocks usually fly to their feeding grounds at night, some feeding during the daytime is undertaken.

Being a southern hemisphere species, their breeding season covers the months of August to March, depending just how far north they are. Their nests are normally hidden away among long grasses.

They are very vocal, especially when in flight, when an incessant clear, low whistled 'whi-whee' echoes out. In flight their wings also produce a whistling sound.

Very aptly named.

A regular feature of most collections and frequently seen on park pools. Only very occasionally seen in a wild state.

WOOD DUCK. L 41 – 50 cm. WS 68 – 74 cm.
Another most colourful duck to rival the mandarin, this time from North America, and sometimes referred to as the Carolina wood duck.

The drake is unmistakable, and almost undescribable with its iridescent dark plumage, white throat and facial markings, combined with an orange and white bill and a crest, all help to make the bird distinctive. The duck resembles very closely a duck mandarin, and great care is required to separate the two.

In a natural state they are usually found in small parties near woodland lakes and rivers, although during winter they do form larger flocks. They are a woodland breeding species, hence their name.

They are a dabbling duck, most buoyant swimmers who upend to feed but rarely dive.

It is understood odd pairs have bred in the UK, although I have never had the pleasure of experiencing this. Unlike the mandarin which now breeds in UK, the wood duck is not accepted as a breeding species, but it is on the British List as a very rare vagrant.

That completes a list of unusual species you may come across, and many are reported from city parks, so when next feeding the ducks, be observant.

CHAPTER III

WHAT IS A BRITISH BIRD?

To get on the British List a bird must meet a specific category to be accepted as a British species, as not all the birds you see are wild; some will be escapees. The British Ornithological Union (the BOU) examines all records and their committee decides what will be accepted. To be accepted a bird must meet a series of categories, and I will list these as from the latest BOU's British List.

Species Categories.
Each species on the British List is placed in one or more categories denoting its status on the list, with only birds from categories A, B, and C being accepted.

In 1997, categorisation was revised to assist protection under national wildlife legislation, especially of naturalised species. Category C was expanded to allow species with different histories of introduction and naturalisation to be distinguished; Category D (not included in the List totals) was reduced in scope, and a Category E (not included in the list) was introduced to enable local and national recorders to monitor escaped species.

Category A.
Species recorded in an apparently natural state at least once since 1st January 1950.
Category B.
Species recorded in an apparently natural state at least once between 1st January 1800 and 31st December 1949, but have not been recoded subsequently.
Category C.
Species that, although introduced, now derive from the resulting self - sustaining populations. As follows:-

C1 Naturalized introduced species – species that have occurred only as a result of introduction, e.g. Egyptian goose.

C2 Naturalized established species – species with established populations resulting from introduction by man, but which also occur in an apparently natural state, e.g. greylag goose.

C3 Naturalized re-established species – species with populations successfully re-established by man in areas of former occurrence, e.g. red kite.

C4 Naturalised feral species – domesticated species with populations in the wild, e.g. feral pigeon.

C5 Vagrant naturalized species – species from established naturalized populations abroad, e.g. possibly some ruddy shelducks occurring in Britain.

C6 Former naturalized species – species formerly placed in C1 whose naturalized populations are no longer self-sustaining or are considered extinct, e.g. Lady Amherst's Pheasant.

Categories not included in the British List.
Category D.
Species that would otherwise appear in Category A except that there is reasonable doubt that they have ever occurred in a natural state.
Category E.
Species recorded as introductions, human-assisted transportees or escapes from captivity, and whose breeding populations (if any) are thought not to be self- sustaining. e.g. canary, peacock etc.

There is a Category F being compiled but we need not concern ourselves with that as it will record species prior to 1800, including fossilised remains. You will not find them in any field guide.

I hope that this will help you understand things more when you read about species categories. Incidentally, the British List currently stands at 623 species, although there are species still under consideration. Many of those may have been recorded only once or twice, but who knows, one year you may be the person who sees such a bird, and your name would go down in birding history. Now there is a thought.

CHAPTER IV

BIRD TERMINOLOGY.

Most hobbies or interests develop a language of their own, and bird study is no different. The very name of bird study, 'ORNITHOLGY', is enough to tell you that. So let us look at some of the biological terms used. I will deal with these alphabetically, an A-Z of terms used.

Abrasion:- The affect of wear on a birds plumage.

Accidental:- A bird which arrives in an area where it does not normally occur.

Albinism:- A total or partial absence of pigment in the feathers of a bird.

Albino:- Completely lacking colour.

Alula:- A small group of feathers situated at the bend of the wing.

Arboreal:- Living among trees, woodpeckers for instance.

Assembly:- A noun used when referring to a group of birds of one kind. Here are a selection of some of these:-

Birds of prey a cast, cormorants a flight, coots a cover. cranes a herd, crows a murder, ducks a raft, when in flight a team, game birds a covey, geese a gaggle when in flight a skein, gulls a squabble jays a band, knots a cluster, lapwings a deceit, larks a bevy, magpies a tiding, mallards a flush, plovers a congregation, quail a drift, ravens a congress, rooks a clamour, snipe a wisp, sparrows a host, starlings a murmuration, swallows a flight, swans a wedge or herd, waders a confusion.

So the next time you hear people refer to a murmuration of starlings, you know what they mean.

Aves;- The scientific name for the family of animal known as birds.

Axillaries:- The feathers at the base of the underside of the wing – the birds 'armpit'.

Beak or Bill:- The projecting jaws of a bird.

Birder:- Originally an American term for someone who watches birds, now in common use in the UK.

Booming:- The call of the bittern.

Busking:- Territorial display of the male mute swan.

Cap:- The colour on the top of the head.

Carpal Joint:- The bend in the bird's wings.

Cere:- The soft fleshy covering at the base of a bird's bill. Most noticeable on birds of prey.

Churring:- The song of a nightjar.

Clipped:- Usually refers to a bird whose primaries have been cut off making it temporary flightless less. But once the primaries grow again it can fly.

Commic Tern:- The combined names of the common tern and arctic tern, used when the bird watcher is uncertain of which he has seen.

Covert:- The name given to the feathers that overlay the base of the wings or tail e.g. wing coverts, tail coverts and ear coverts. The colour of these can be very important when identifying similar species. .

Crepuscular:- Active at dusk and dawn, not during the night.

Culman:- The ridge on the top of the upper mandible of the bill.

Diurnal:- Active during daylight.

Drake:- A male duck.

Drumming:- The sound caused by woodpeckers when raining a succession of blows on a branch or trunk of a tree.

Eclipse:- The period when a bird's breeding plumage is replaced by duller colours. Usually relates to male ducks.

Eyrie:- The nest of a bird of prey, especially used in relationship to eagles.

Fall:- The sudden appearance of a considerable number of migrant species.

Feral:- Birds which were once captive and are now breeding in a wild state. e.g. feral pigeons, greylag and Canada geese being examples.

Flanks:- The side of a bird.

Gander:- a male goose.

Hybrid:- The result of interbreeding by two different species. Rare in the wild, but occurs to captive birds more frequently.

Irruption:- The term applied to irregular migration movements of certain species dependent on a particular food when it becomes in short supply.

Juvenile:- A young bird, at the stage of obtaining its first full plumage of true feathers.

Lek:- Originally used to describe an assembly of black grouse, the males only. Now used for groups of some other species, when males congregate.

Lifer:- An expression used by bird watchers when they see a bird for the very first time.

Lobed:- When water birds have toes separately fringed by lobes, not webbed. Coots, great crested grebes etc.

Loon:- The north American name for divers.

Lore:- The area between the base of the upper mandible and the eyes.

Mandible:- The jaws of a bird. The adjective 'upper' and 'lower' is added where necessary..

Melanism:- The opposite to albinism, being an excess of dark pigment in the plumage.

Mew Gull:- A local name for the common gull, frequently used in the U.S.A.

Migration:- The regular movement of birds between alternate areas they inhabit at different times of the year. i.e. breeding and non-breeding.

Mirrors:- The term used for the white patches seen on the primaries of some of the gulls.

Moult:- The periodic shedding and renewal of a bird's plumage. All birds moult at least once a year, some as much as three times.

Moustachial:- The name for a dark streak in some plumages running from the base of the bill.

Nocturnal:- Active at night.

Oology:- The scientific name for the study of bird's eggs.

Ornithology:- The scientific study of birds.

Overshooting:- When a bird travels beyond its normal range or breeding area when migrating.

Palmate:- Having three toes connected by webs.

Passage Migration:-A bird which only passes through an area on migration, does not stay.

Passerines:- Generally described as perching or singing birds, which covers well over half of all the world's known birds.

Pinioned:- Relating mainly to ducks where the flight feathers are removed and the bird can no longer fly.

Primary:- The large feathers on a bird's wing which stretch from the carpal joint to the wing tips, without them a bird would have great difficulty in flying.

Race:- A sub-division within a species, usually determined by slight differences in colour and measurements of a bird. Also known as a sub-species.

Raft:- Collective term for a number of birds together when on the sea.

Range:- The part of the world over which a bird extends, both where breeding and migrating.

Raptor:- The term used for birds of prey.

Resident:- A bird that remains in the country it is was raised throughout its life.

Sawbill:- The term for ducks which have tooth-like serrations on their bills.

Scapulars:- The feathers above the shoulder.

Secondary:- Any one of the flight feathers on the forewing, as contrasted with the primaries.

Sedentary:- A bird which rarely moves far from the area in which it was raised.

Shank:- The term used for the whole or part of the leg.

Shorebird:- The North American name for waders.

Speculum:- A patch of bright colour on the wings, usually on the secondaries. As the blue patch on a mallard's wings.

Stoop:- Usually associated with a bird of prey's rapid dive, especially the peregrine.

Sub-species:- Another expression for 'race'.

Summer visitor:- A much used, although in my opinion incorrect, for a species which is only seen during the summer months when it is breeding. I believe this is completely wrong; they are not visitors, they are returning migrants, coming home to where they were born.

Supercillium:- A mark above the eye, usually a stripe.

Talons:- The claws of a bird of prey.

Tiercel:- The term used for a male falcon.

Tippet:- The elongated facial feathers found on grebes.

Vagrant:- A bird which has wandered outside its normal range.

Yaffle:- A name associated with the green woodpecker, derived from its laughing, yaffle-like call.

That is a selection of expressions made by birders, many of which are part of the descriptions used in field guides.

CHAPTER V

WHERE TO SEE AND LEARN ABOUT BIRDS

Bird watching is a hobby which can be done alone or with company, and if new to the game I always suggest membership of a bird watching club where the help from experienced bird watchers is available, and willingly given in most circumstances. To start off with, membership of the RSPB Youth Membership Scheme is suggested. This is an ideal introduction to birds and membership also brings you free admission into all the RSPB nature reserves.

No matter where you live an RSPB reserve is never too far away. They have over 200 reserves to choose from, and some of these are nationally important, and thanks to the RSPB they are secure from interference and development. They will always remain sanctuaries for birds and all other forms of wildlife.

Most counties have their own wildlife trusts and they too have nature reserves which can be visited by members free of charge, and some of these rival the RSPB for the variety of wildlife they support. Membership of your local trust will quickly introduce you to local sites which you probably did not know existed. Here you can quickly get to know many of your local bird watchers who can be useful in the future.

There are also the more specialised societies, the Wildfowl and Wetlands Trust for instance. They have centres which not only attract large numbers of wildfowl and other birds, they also have collections of captive birds which enables you to get closer to them than you will ever do in the wild.

Finally, there are many local bird watching clubs which is a very good place to start. I live in Staffordshire and locally we have the West Midlands Bird Club which covers Warwickshire, Staffordshire, Worcestershire and the West Midlands, and just over the county boundary is the Derbyshire Ornithological Society. They both operate a hotline which on a daily basis informs you of the top birds which have been seen in the area, so you can try to experience them if you so wish. Some also have their own nature reserves. The West Midlands Bird Club certainly has, and members are allowed here for free. Addresses for local societies can be found at your local library and on 'Google'.

Enough about bird societies. Let us now look at literature, field guides in particular. There are many books written about birds and bird watching, I have written them myself, but a field guide is totally different; it is this which will help you identify any bird you may see, and there are many of them, both books and birds. The important thing is to have one which will fit your pocket; many are too large and heavy and are of more use at home.

To start with, guides to the birds of Great Britain and Europe, which many are, cover many birds you are unlikely to see, especially if you are a newcomer to the hobby. The ideal guide for the beginner is the RSPB *Handbook of British Birds*. This does exactly what it says on the cover; it covers the 270 species that either breed in the UK or are seen here regularly, plus a further 26 rare migrants or vagrants that occur less frequently, but might be encountered by the lucky observer. That is 296 species as compared with the 623 on the current British List. The species dealt with in this publication provide more information than that in any field guide, which usually only concentrate on identification and distribution. A first class publication.

As your experience grows and you may holiday abroad, then a field guide which also includes the birds found in the appropriate area becomes more a necessity to enable you to identify what you see, and there are three I use.

My oldest is the *Hamlyn Guide to Birds of Britain and Europe*, by Bertel Bruun. This book was first published 1971, and it has travelled Europe with me. It covers 530 birds in colour, so only the oldest or more recent additions are not covered. It also fits the pocket. I have yet to see a bird in Europe not included in it.

The guide favoured by many birders is the *Collins Bird Guide*; this was first published in 1999, and the information contained within its covers provides all the information required to identify any species at anytime of the year. This is important as a bird's plumage goes through several stages during a year; a bird in summer plumage may look entirely different in winter plumage, and juveniles look different to adults. The only problem with this book is that many of the illustrations are small, and the 448 pages make it too large for any pocket. To compensate for this I purchased the large format edition which now sits proudly on my book shelf.

My favourite field guide is, however, *Birds of Europe* by Lars Jonsson, first published 1996 by Christopher Helm/ A & C Black. This has over 2,500 illustrations and comprises 560 pages. Once again it is too large for the pocket, but when I drove it was a constant companion in my car, and is still the guide I use mostly when at home. The quality of Lars Jonsson's illustrations is unlikely to be beaten, these were done by a bird watcher, not just an artist.

Those are just my thoughts, but when buying your field guide, do look through it closely to make sure it provides you with the information you require. There are no bad field guides, it is just that some are better than others, but it is your choice.

As I mentioned in my introduction, optics are necessary, and here I will not try to influence you as price is a big question. If however you wish to buy, do try them out first and remember that weight is an important feature. You are likely to carry them about all day, and with telescopes a tripod or hide clamp is a necessity. With binoculars I suggest buying a pair with a fixed magnification i.e. 8x or 10x, I would suggest you do not go above 10x, and with a telescope a zoom lens is very useful. My telescope has a zoom from 20x to 60x, and when viewing over long distances this brings the bird into view far better. But always remember the one thing I have said, try before you buy!

That brings me to the end. As the title illustrated, my hope is to introduce you to a life long hobby that can be enjoyed at whatever level you wish, be that as an expert or just a bird lover, the choice is yours. There is no pressure, birds are just to be enjoyed, and the only two things required are patience and respect. They are things of beauty and when studied closely they also have personality, and can be seen almost everywhere.

Before I close, I wish to thank my friend and fellow birder, Evelyn Syer, for her help in making this possible.

Go forth and enjoy.

Happy birding.

BRIAN GEORGE.

Previous publications by the author.

Englsih Churchyard Flora. Curlew Countryside Publications.
The Birdwatchers Day List, co-edited with Chaz Mason. Curlew
Countryside Publications.
The Flora of a Gravel Pit. The University of Birmingham.
A Journal of a Year in the Life of a BLUE BADGE BIRDER. The Derby
Books Publishing Co.
SEARCHING an autobiography of a birder, in two volumes. Olympia
Publishers.